ASPEN POTPOURRI

A 50-Year Collection of Aspen Recipes and Ideas

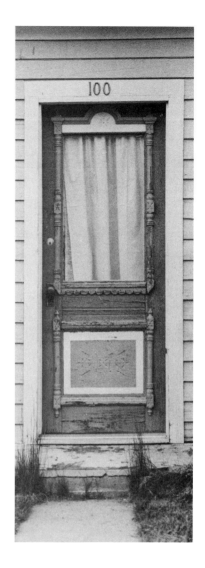

Mary Eshbaugh Hayes

Photographed and Collected

by

MARY ESHBAUGH HAYES

FIRST EDITION — 1968
SECOND EDITION — 1971
THIRD EDITION — 1975
FOURTH EDITION — 1990
FIFTH EDITION — 2002

ADDITIONAL COPIES:
MARY ESHBAUGH HAYES, Box 497, Aspen, Colorado 81611

Published by Aspen Potpourri ✳ Printed by Crested Butte Printing
ISBN 0-9641960-3-4

FOREWORD

A town is its people. The houses with their doors, windows and gingerbread. The gardens. Even the relics. They all reflect the people who live in that town.

Potpourri is a mixture…and this book is a mixture of Aspen…its people, its places and its food.

Aspen Potpourri grew out of the "Around Aspen" column I write for *The Aspen Times*. I always felt the most interesting thing about Aspen is its mix of people. Like my "Around Aspen" column, Aspen Potpourri includes a potpourri of Aspen people…some old timers, some newcomers, some jet setters, some artists, some writers, some celebrities, some musicians, some truck drivers and cat-skinners, some chefs and some just good cooks. The people range from children to grandparents.

Most of the photographs were taken during the 1960s, the 1970s, the 1980s and 1990s. There are even a few from the 1950s and some from 2001 and 2002 so the book actually spans 50 years in Aspen.

I came to Aspen in 1952 to work for *The Aspen Times* as a reporter-photographer. When I married silversmith Jim Hayes in 1953, I couldn't cook. People gave me recipes. They came to the house and taught me how to make soup and bake bread.

Jim and I had five kids so I stayed home for several years. However, I had a photography business documenting events, families, weddings, doing portraits. With the "Around Aspen" column, I was always taking photos at galas. I began to see a way to combine the photos with the recipes and ideas that Aspenites had shared with me over the years.

Our children were a great part of the book. When they were little ones, we called it "cookbooking." I would telephone someone and say were were coming to take their photo and get their recipe. The kids and I would ride over on our bicycles. The person we'd chosen would cook up their recipe…and we'd all all have tea or dinner. The kids loved it!

Over the years the kids grew up and left home. In 1972 I went back to work full time at *The Aspen Times,* first as a reporter-photographer, then the editor. In 1992 I retired and now just write "Around Aspen" and some features. And I keep on "cookbooking."

There are two rather different sections in the book. In addition to recipes for food, a section of "Idea Recipes" explains some of the things Aspenites do. There is also a section on "Local Wild Edibles" which gives recipes for the Rocky Mountain wild berries and mushrooms.

This is the fifth edition of *Aspen Potpourri*. The first was published in 1968, another in 1971, another in 1975 and another in 1990. With each addition, I added people and their recipes. I never took anyone out. So the book has become a part of Aspen history.

This longtime favorite is back, with 50 additional and new photos and recipes of Aspenites. The book now has some 316 pages.

Some of the people are no longer in Aspen. However, all the people in this book gave something of themselves to Aspen…and will always be a part of Aspen.

Mary Eshbaugh Hayes — Springtime 2002

Ethel McCabe's window.

STUART MACE
Serves hearty meals at his Toklat in Aspen restaurant
— and is famed for his Husky dog sled tours in the
high country above Toklat in Ashcroft.

The old hotel in Ashcroft.

MULESKINNER'S DELIGHT

This recipe was given to Stuart by Joe Sawyer who got it from "The Blue
Mirror Saloon" in Ashcroft. It is an old miner's drink that "will cure anything."

Put the teakettle on. Have big heavy mug with no handle. Preheat mug
with hot water. Pour water out.

Into mug put: A full jigger of straight mellow well aged bourbon. A full
jigger of blackberry brandy. One rounded teaspoonful of brown sugar. Fill up
mug with boiling water and stir.

Put your feet up on the cabin stove and warm your feet, warm your hands
around the mug, and warm your insides with the "Muleskinner's Delight." Not
recommended on an empty stomach.

GLUHWEIN

This hot spiced wine is a favorite after skiing drink. One cup boiling water to which add a thick slice of lemon, 4 cloves, and two cinnamon sticks — boil 5 minutes. Then add two cups of wine and sugar to taste. Reheat, but do not boil. Use any heavy red wine, Marca Petri is good.

SEPP UHL
Skier, artist and woodcarver.

Bavarian chest handcrafted and painted by Sepp.

ICE COFFEE

For 8 cups of cold coffee, use 1 pint of chocolate ice cream, mix, put in 1 teaspoon vanilla extract. Fill into high glasses and top with whipped cream. For special, put in rum.

TONI UHL

When his mother, Gretl Uhl, gives a summer garden party, Toni helps by whipping up these coolers. Like his father, Sepp, Toni is artistic.

JACK DE PAGTER

A member of the Mountain Rescue Group - Jack instructs a group of teenagers in rock climbing.

BISCHOP WYN

Guests at Holland House come down from the slopes on wintry afternoons and find Jack brewing this hot wine.

1 gallon dark red California wine
½ gallon water
1 teaspoon whole cloves
2 teaspoons cinnamon or stick cinnamon
½ cup raisins
1 orange, sliced sugar to taste

Mix altogether in big pot. Heat, but do not boil.

BARBI BENTON'S APRICOT LIQUEUR

Note: This recipe takes three months to mature ingredients.

    1 pound Rock Candy
    1 pound dried apricots
    ½ gallon Vodka

Buy top quality apricots and Vodka to assure delicious liqueur. Rock Candy usually comes on strings or sticks which must be removed.

In a large, wide-mouthed jar (Barbi uses one that is made for sun-tea) combine rock candy and vodka. Cover and let stand for about one week (or until sugar has dissolved).

Strain the liquid into another container to remove strings or sticks, then pour the sweetened vodka back into the original jar and add the apricots.

It will take several months for the liqueur to become mellow. After three months, it is usually ready for consumption, but the longer it stands, the better it tastes. It is at its best when it is a year old.

When it is smooth enough to serve to company, put the liquid **and** the apricots in an attractive liqueur bottle that has a mouth wide enough for you to remove the apricots with a fork. The apricots look beautiful in a bottle and taste fabulous. Don't hesitate to float an apricot in each liqueur glass. The liqueur and the apricots make a wonderful topping for ice cream and custard.

BARBI BENTON
Dancer-actress Barbi Benton and her husband, real estate developer George Gradow, are very involved with Aspen arts groups. They often give gala parties for the Aspen Art Museum and DanceAspen.

PAUL SOLDNER

Paul is one of America's most famous artists working in clay. His handbuilt home-studio just outside Aspen is a craftsman's wonder. And it is solar heated. Paul is as famous for his homemade wines. On a lucky day he might serve you homemade soup and bread with a glass of his red raspberry or rhubarb wine.

RED RASPBERRY WINE

This is a recipe for one gallon. For more, just multiply the ingredients.

½ of a pound raspberries (or two of those little dry pints)

gallon of water

2¼ pounds of white cane sugar

1 cup raisins

½ teaspoon instant tea

juice of ½ lemon including skins. Juice, but throw it all in.

1 campden tablet (a measured amount of sulfite) from any wine store. Be warned...some people are allergic to sulfites.

One wine yeast (better than baker's yeast). Or a champagne yeast makes it clear and cleaner. Also available from wine store.

First Day: Put berries in clean stainless or glass container and crush with baseball bat (or feet).

Then heat (almost to a boil) ¾ of the water, holding ¼ back.

Add when hot to the berries.

Then add everything except the yeast. It will die from high temperatures.

Cover the container with cloth to keep out fruit flies.

Second day: When room temperature, add the yeast to berries and stir and cover again.

Every day stir once or twice.

Fifth day: Strain into glass jug and fit with fermentation trap (again available from wine store).

Every two to three months rack: Siphon wine from that jug into new clean jug. Careful not to disturb sediment at bottom and then replace trap. Make sure water in trap never evaporates.

When wine is completely clear, until sparkling clear (varies around six months to a year) there will be no more activity and no more sediment. Then bottle in clear bottles and cork.

RHUBARB WINE

Equal parts of rhubarb to sugar.

2¼ lbs. of rhubarb, chopped as for pie

2¼ lbs. sugar

First day: Cover rhubarb with sugar and stir, stand 24 hours (be careful not to go over 24 hours).

Wash in one gallon of hot water to dissolve sugar (you can now use the rhubarb for pies) because all you need now is the liquid.

Add one of the campden tablets

1 cup chopped-up raisins

skip the lemon

½ teaspoon tea

When cool, add one champagne yeast

Follow same procedure as for red raspberry wine.

On the fifth day strain into bottles.

This makes a nice dry wine. You can cut down on amount of rhubarb if you don't want such a rhubarby taste.

Paul says that wine-making is the world's cheapest hobby...but one enjoys the fruits of your labor.

SUZY'S SKI SMOOTHIE

Serves 2

1 cup frozen mixed berries of your choice
   organic if you can
1 cup rice milk
1 banana, organic if possible
2 tablespoons soft tofu
1 teaspoon molasses (for arthritis prevention)

Blend in blender.
Can add more rice milk to taste.

Optional ski longevity additives

add ½ teaspoon spirulina powder
2 tablespoons Ultimate Meal
2 tablespoons ground flax seed
1 tablespoon Knox gelatin (for joints)

SUZY CHAFFEE

Suzy Chaffee was the star in the movie, "Fire and Ice," an Aspen love story. She was the Captain of the 1968 Olympic downhill ski team, inventor of Ski Ballet and three-time world freestyle champion.

Suzy Chaffee and Northern Ute Renessa Ridley fly like eagles down Buttermilk Mountain. With Indian Unity Leader Alden Naranjo, Suzy co-founded the Native Voices Foundation, working on programs that expose American Indian youth to winter sports. Photo courtesy of Connie Baxter Marlow.

THE ASPEN CRUD

from Tony Di Lucia, manager of The Hotel Jerome

Throughout the Hotel Jerome's rich history, the Jerome Bar or J-Bar as it is locally known, has been one of the town's most popular gathering spots. From the silver miners of the late 19th Century, who would belly up to the bar to celebrate their good fortune, to today's Hollywood stars who celebrate a fortune of another kind, the J-Bar continues to be a place of good times and good drink.

In fact, the J-Bar's celebrated drink-the now infamous "Aspen Crud" is steeped in Aspen and Hotel Jerome history. Like bars across America, the J-Bar was converted to a soda fountain during Prohibition. During World War II, the 10th Mountain Division boarded at the hotel and concocted the famed drink, adding several shots of liquor, usually bourbon, to a rich milkshake blended at the J-Bar fountain-a spirited example of American ingenuity.

TONY DI LUCIA

Tony Di Lucia always gave a luncheon honoring Judith Child in the garden at the Hotel Jerome during the *Food & Wine Magazine* Classic in Aspen.

5 "rounded" 1⅓ oz. Scoops of French Vanilla Ice Cream (Hotel Jerome's preference is Haagen-Dazs)

3 "perfect pours" 1 oz. Shots of Bourbon (Hotel Jerome's preference is Jack Daniels)

Place scoops of Ice Cream in a blender and add shots of Bourbon. Blend for several seconds until a perfect creamy consistency is obtained,

Prepares one serving

The Hotel Jerome

Helen Gloor and her kids

A Viking.

Three favorite ladies: left to right are Louiva Stapleton, Lena Van Loon, and Laura Durrenberger.

CHICKEN LIVER PATE

1 lb. chicken livers
1 large onion, slightly chopped
¼ cup chicken broth

⅛ cup brandy
¼ cup sherry or cognac

Simmer until livers are pink and firm. Empty mixture into blender, including liquid. Add

½ teaspoon curry powder
½ teaspoon paprika

1 tablespoon Worcestershire sauce
salt and ground pepper (to taste)

Cover and blend. Uncover and, chunk by chunk, add one stick of butter. Then add about 2 tablespoons of sour cream, and 2 tablespoons of cream cheese. Blend well. Chill and serve on crackers.

SALLY DALE
With her ballet class.

ULLA
Aspen's beautiful Swede.

JANSSONS FRESTELSE (Johnson's Temptation)

6 medium size boiling potatoes
2 medium yellow or red onions
1 can anchovy filets (long ones,
    not rolled ones)

half pint of whipping cream
    (or half and half)
1 stick butter or margarine

Butter your pan — a baking pan or frying pan — sprinkle butter with bread crumbs. Slice potatoes raw, like a fine french fry and cut up onions in thin slices.

Make one layer of potatoes, completely cover bottom of pan, then one layer of onions, sprinkle around. Take half of can of anchovies and sprinkle around. Then make second layer of these ingredients, leaving a few potatoes for the very top. Pour on cream and dabs of butter and bread crumbs. Bake for one to one and a half hours at 350 to 400 degrees until the top is browned. Cut into small pieces and let your guests serve themselves from the pan.

HUBERT ERHARD
Brings Austrian charm to Aspen.

GOLDEN HORN APPETIZER

Start with a thin French pancake made of flour, egg, milk and salt — consistency should be fairly thin so as to barely coat the spoon. Blend well so there are no lumps.

Melt some butter in frying pan, allow to get medium hot, pour from one edge some of the mixture into frying pan — so mixture covers evenly bottom of frying pan about 1/16 of an inch thick. Slowly cook on one side, over medium heat, to a light golden color — turn with spatula and finish other side to same color.

Put pancake aside on a plate, then mix some canned tuna fish, cubed boiled shrimp, some lump crab meat, and steamed oysters (all items may be used out of cans). Season well with lemon juice and garlic powder.

Then place pancake flat into individual casserole, fill with seafood mixture, and roll up pancake like a sausage. (Place roll so flap is under.) Put into 325 degree oven for 5 to 10 minutes so mixture and casserole get hot — be careful and not dry out.

Heat up Campbell cheddar cheese soup, follow directions except use milk instead of water. Finish the sauce with red pepper or hot sauce and dry sherry wine to taste. Pour over pancake in casserole so pancake is completely covered with cheese sauce. Put back in oven, increase heat a little, leave until cheese sauce begins to bubble up on the edge, serve immediately. Place hot casserole on a dinner plate covered with napkin to prevent sliding. Can be prepared several to a large casserole or individually as at "The Golden Horn."

Snowfalls deep and white.

YVONNE THOMAS
The artists' artist — with one of her paintings.

PEPPERS PROVENCALE (an hors d'oeuvre)

Take 10 green peppers, wash, put under broiler until skins are partially singed, let cool and remove thin skin. Cut each pepper in eight long sections, removing all seeds. Place in dish horizontally and pour over the peppers a dressing of olive oil, vinegar, salt and pepper with generous amount of chopped garlic and parsley.

LORENZO SEMPLE, JR.

A screenwriter who lives in Aspen and works in a funky office in The Elks Building, Lorenzo Semple is famous for his scripts for "King Kong" and the television series of "Batman."

CAVIAR PIE

Lorenzo's wife, Joyce Semple, tells me she got this recipe from Lois Dwan, food editor of the **Los Angeles Times** who sometimes shared with friends the recipes she found...that were too good to print. This is one of those recipes and Joyce says Lorenzo stole it from her.

This is a very easy appetizer that never fails to win cheers of the best sort; that is to say, people cry, "Oh no, that's not on my diet!" —and end up pigging out on the delicious stuff.

8 mashed hard boiled eggs
¾ stick melted butter
½ pt. sour cream
1 tb. grated onion
1 4-oz. jar black caviar
1 baked 9-inch pie shell

Combine butter and eggs. Press into pie shell, sprinkle with onion. Spread sour cream and stick in freezer for 1 hour. Take out, spread caviar on top, and serve. That's it.

NOTE: If you are the sort of Aspen developer who gets Seven Million dollar checks from anonymous friends who won't be identified, by all means indulge yourself in Beluga malassol caviar. Otherwise, use the truly inexpensive black Lumpfish variety. It's just as good.

ALICE'S HOT ARTICHOKE DIP

One 14-oz. can artichoke hearts

One 4-oz. can chopped green chiles

¾ cup mayonaise (light)

¼ cup sour cream

1 cup grated parmesan cheese

Chop artichoke hearts. Mix all ingredients together. Heat in microwave — high power two to three minutes and stir after each minute until cheese has melted.

Serve with crackers or tortilla chips.

To cook in traditional oven, heat at 350 degrees, stirring once or twice until cheese has melted.

LITA HELLER

Lita is the original of Aspen's black-tie hostesses. Bursting on the Aspen social scene in the early 1970s, she has raised funds for all of Aspen's arts groups...DanceAspen, the Aspen Music Festival, and the Aspen Art Museum.

Aspen's yellow roses

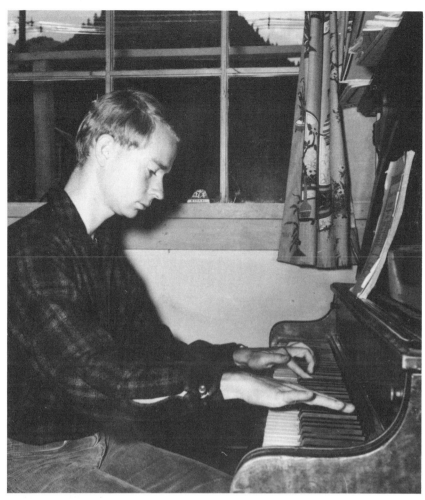

BRUCE BERGER
Poet, pianist and world traveler.

BITTER LEMON SALAD DRESSING

½ cup cider vinegar	salt
½ cup Bitter Lemon	whole ground pepper
¼ cup salad oil	oregano
	grated parmesan cheese

Mix the vinegar, salad oil and Bitter Lemon together, stirring well. Shake small amounts of the salt, whole ground pepper and oregano into the mixture. Add enough grated parmesan cheese for the liquid to attain a slight texture, stirring vigorously. A bit of parmesan cheese may also be shaken over the salad after the dressing is applied.

Note: After using ½ cup of Bitter Lemon you will still have most of the bottle left over. This need not be wasted but may be pleasurably mixed with smaller amounts of gin, bourbon or vodka. It makes excellent refreshment and will help console you if the salad dressing comes out wrong.

THOUSAND ISLAND DRESSING

Put all ingredients in bowl and stir well, until dressing is an even pink.

4 tablespoons catsup

8 oz. bottle (1 cup) mayonnaise (Miracle Whip)

2 eggs, hardboiled and cut up in tiny pieces

about 6 sweet chip pickles or 3 small sweet pickles, cut in tiny pieces

2 tablespoons pickle juice

PAULINE PEDERSEN
A teacher and seeker of knowledge.

Jim's famous Aspenleaf pin.

JIM HAYES

Aspen's earthmoving silversmith — in summers he drives giant earthmovers and in winters he handmakes gold and silver jewelry.

ROQUEFORT DRESSING

Into blender put these ingredients:

2½ oz. package of Roquefort cheese **or** 4 oz. package of Blue cheese

12 oz. (about 1½ cups) cultured sour cream

juice of half a lemon

1 clove garlic, chopped tiny

pepper and salt to taste

½ cup milk

3 tablespoons mayonnaise (Miracle Whip)

Blend these ingredients well and just before serving over salad add 3 chopped green onions, including some of the green stems. Do **not** blend in the onions or they will discolor the dressing — just stir in with spoon. Refrigerate any left over — good for two or three days.

Picnicking in the shade of Jim's high speed scraper on the Reudi dam job.

VANESSA WALLNER
Has birds, fish, turtles, hamsters, a kitten, dogs.

A SALAD CHILDREN LIKE

Children often prefer a salad without dressing — and this is one Vanessa invented for her family.

Place lettuce leaves in your salad bowl so they cover the sides of the bowl like a nest. Peel and slice apples and oranges and mix well — making sure orange juice gets on the apples so they won't discolor. Then place the apple and orange mixture into the lettuce nest and cover with a bit of shredded lettuce — serve.

JO AND BEN BIANCO

The first time we met Jo and Ben — they were walking down our street holding hands. Ben is a Designer, worked here for Herbert Bayer, and Jo is a writer.

A GREEN AND NUTTY SALAD

½ lb. package chopped pecans
1 pint cottage cheese

1 can crushed pineapple, drained
2 packages lime jello (mix as directed)

Mix altogether and put in refrigerator to set. Then sit down and have a cocktail — Ben suggests this summer drink.

CAMPARI a la BIANCO

For each 8 to 10 oz. glass
1 jigger Campari (a very bitter vermouth)

1 tablespoon Grenadine

Fill glass with club soda and ice and mix.

ARDITH WARE

Her summertime hobby is to poke and dig around old mine dumps and ghost towns — adding to one of the best bottle collections in the area.

STRAWBERRY-PINEAPPLE SALAD

2 packages cherry gelatin
2 cups hot water
1 #2 can crushed pineapple
1 medium box frozen strawberries
3 bananas (crushed)
1 carton sour cream (12 oz.)

Add hot water to gelatin and stir well. Mix in strawberries, pineapple and bananas. Put half of mixture in mold (or individual goblets) and chill till set. Add sour cream, by spreading on top — then add balance of fruit and gelatin mixture and chill until completely set.

Some of the treasures Ardith found while digging for bottles.

The children dig for crucibles — used in the mining days to assay the gold and silver ore.

And fill them with wax and wick — to sell to the shops as crucible candles.

GRITS AND GREENS

Any mixture of frozen or fresh chopped greens. Add drained hominy, white or yellow or both. Mix with a little fat of choice or crumbled bacon, ham or sausage. Heat until hot.

ROBERT G. MARSH

Bob is the owner of the Half House.

The Half House

CAESAR SALAD

Two heads of Romaine, dried and crisped

Mash two cloves of garlic in a wooden bowl

Add anchovy paste to thoroughly cover
    inside of bowl

Break up Romaine in bowl

Add yolk of one egg and toss

Squeeze juice of one to two lemons over greens. Add parmesan cheese, oil and dry mustard to taste. Toss again. Season with salt and pepper and add croutons to top if you wish.

JUDY DOWS

She is the Wineglass Weaver.

GUACAMOLE DIP

      6 avocados
    ½ tomato
    ½ onion
      2 tablespoons garden fresh hot
            sauce which is made with a
            combination of the following:
            tomatoes
            water
            onions
            chili peppers
            vinegar
            salt
            dash of cayenne pepper, chili
                powder and pepper.
The avocados can be put into a blender, or cut into tiny pieces with knife or fork. The onion, tomato, and garden fresh hot sauce must be diced. Stir all the ingredients together and dip with fritos or doritos.

JAYNE SMITH

In her shop, 20th Century Fox, Jayne sells handmade, original designs in clothing.

RODDEY BURDINE

A prize winning costume designer for movies (he won the Academy Award for designs in The Great Gatsby), Roddey has been involved in Aspen's 1976 Centennial-Bicentennial events.

POPPY SEED DRESSING

Mix in blender:

1½ cups sugar
 1 tablespoon dry mustard
 2 teaspoons salt
 3 tablespoons lemon juice
⅔ cup white vinegar
 3 tablespoons onion juice

Add 2 cups salad oil slowly while blending, then blend at high speed for about 5 minutes. Then fold in 2½ tablespoons poppy seeds. Will keep in refrigerator for weeks.

Add mayonnaise to this for a great potato salad dressing. Especially good as is on fruit salad.

ENSALADA DE NOCHEBUENA (CHRISTMAS EVE SALAD)

4 beets

1 large radish

2 jicamas

2 apples

2 firm bananas

2 limes

2 oranges

1 pomegranate

peanuts

pine nuts

honey

vinegar

beet juice

salt

Slice cooked or canned beets. Slice radish. Cut all else into squares. Peel and crumble pomegranate. Add nuts. Combine vinegar and salt to honey, with beet juice for color and toss.

EDITH EVANS

Living in Old Mexico for many years, Edith Evans was a famous lady bullfighter.

This painting of a prize bull hangs in one of Aspen's barns in the ranchlands.

TOFU—UMEBOSHI—DILL SALAD DRESSING

1 block tofu, steamed
1 teaspoon dill
1 tablespoon umeboshi pickled plum paste
1 clove garlic chopped (optional)
or 3 green onions chopped (optional)
1 avocado (optional)

Blend all ingredients in blender until smooth. Use dressing over salad, vegetables, or cooked grains. Delicious on brown rice.

NANCY PFISTER

An environmentalist, Nancy has started several organic gardens in the Aspen area.

TERRY'S DIET POTATO SALAD

2 lbs. potatoes (about 10 medium potatoes) that are boiled and cut up

3 cups diced celery

1 cup diced green onion

3 cups chopped hard-boiled egg whites

(option...can add a few hard-boiled egg yokes as desired)

Mix all the above and then add Seven Seas Viva Italian Dressing to taste. Usually takes about 1/2 or 2/3 of one large bottle.

TERRY BUTLER

A former television star who had her own program in Old Mexico, Terry now owns the Ultimate Result Gymnasium in Aspen. Blond, slender and vivacious, she is her own best advertisement for the gym.

GUN AGELL

The leading fashion model in the 1950s (countless covers on **Vogue**), Gun
had an interior design business many years in Aspen and became known
as a fabulous hostess. She now has a llama farm and healing center at the
foot of Mt. Ranier in Washington State.

CAULIFLOWER SALAD

Serves four to six.

   1 head cauliflower

   salt

   6 anchovy fillets, finely chopped

   25 black olives, pitted and chopped

   chopped parsley

   1 garlic clove, finely chopped

   2 tablespoons finely chopped capers

   6 tablespoons olive oil

   2 tablespoons red wine vinegar

   freshly ground black pepper

   1. Remove green leaves from cauliflower, trim stem and cut off any bruised spots.
Break or cut cauliflower into flowerets and poach in lightly-salted water for about 5
minutes. Drain and place in a bowl of cold salted water until ready to use. Drain
again. Dry thoroughly.

   2. Mix finely chopped anchovies, olives, parsley, garlic, and capers with olive oil
and red wine vinegar. Add cauliflowerets and season with salt and freshly ground
black pepper to taste. Arrange in a bowl.

CLAYTON and DONNA HAYES and Son, JAMES PAUL

Clayt is a native-born Aspenite, hiking and ski-instructing like so many of the local kids. He and Donna lived and worked in Aspen several years after their marriage...Clayt as a structural engineer and Donna as a teacher in Aspen Elementary School. They now live in Honolulu, Hawaii, where Donna grew up, and go to the beach instead of the mountain.

On the beach in Hawaii.

CHINESE CHICKEN SALAD

    1 head Chinese cabbage, washed and chopped

    4 chicken breasts, boneless and skinless

    1 bunch green onions, chopped

    1 cup celery, chopped

    1 package dry saimin noodles, crumbled

    ¼ cup sesame seeds

    flour, vegetable oil, sesame oil

    won ton chips or won ton pi (wrappers)

Tropics Oriental Dressing, or make your own dressing as follows:

    4 tablespoons lemon juice

    4 tablespoons shoyu

    4 teaspoons sugar

    pepper

    1 teaspoon salt

    8 teaspoons sesame oil

    ½ teaspoon celery salt

    1 teaspoon Chinese five spice

    8 tablespoons salad oil

              Mix well

Coat chicken breasts with flour and fry in vegetable oil until golden brown. Slice into strips.

If using fresh won ton wrappers, cut into strips and deep fry until golden brown. Drain on a paper towel.

Crumble saimin noodles to bite-size pieces. Brown in sesame oil and add sesame seeds just before finishing. Drain on a paper towel.

Combine all ingredients and toss with bottled dressing or your own dressing as listed here. Serves four hungry adults.

ELIZABETH WALLNER WITH DAUGHTER ALEXI

Liz's home is a wonderland of children and greenery everywhere — and she is one of those excellent English secretaries.

ENGLISH CHUTNEY SAUCE

To be used with meats — especially lamb.

4 lbs. tomatoes

1 teaspoon mustard seed

2 teaspoons allspice

½ teaspoon cayenne pepper

1¼ cups sugar

1 teaspoon salt

2 cups vinegar (1 white, 1 apple cider vinegar)

About 1 lb. apples

Peel tomatoes. Tie spices in a bag and add to tomatoes and chopped apples. Boil until reduced to a pulp. Then add salt, sugar and vinegar. Continue boiling until as firm a consistency as desired (at least an hour). Put up in sterilized bottles and seal.

MARCIA LEVINS COWEE
One of Aspen's resident artists, Marcia paints in acrylics and watercolors and also creates works in handmade paper. Her studio overlooks Hunter Creek.

GREAT—GRANDMOTHER'S CHILI SAUCE

20 large tomatoes
12 large peaches
12 large pears
1 large bunch celery
4 red bell peppers
3 green peppers
6 large onions
3 cups cider vinegar
2 pound boxes brown sugar
3 tablespoons salt
1 tablespoon cinnamon
1 tablespoon dill spice
May add hot chilis
Chop and cook all ingredients one hour.
This is good with ham, chicken, on hamburgers, etc.

JANE CICERO LABELLE
Jane started designing her Bearware clothes for children in Aspen and now she sells her line nationally.

MISO SOUP

½ cup barley

1 small head cabbage, cut up

2 onions, chopped

4 carrots, cut up

¼ cup tamari

Cover above with water and simmer until tender, at least 90 minutes. Add water as needed.

Add about ¼ cup red miso (or to taste). Miso blends in better if you add some soup stock to it to make a smooth paste and then add to soup.

Simmer a few minutes. Remove from heat and add about ½ cup sour cream, stirring well.

Serve with warm whole-wheat tortillas.

KATHY LAMM

It was life in a tipi in Lenado for many years for Kathy and she bakes her own bread and makes her own soups. She is a weaver, and colors her own wools with dyes made from native plants. Here she is with daughters Chamisa and Harumi (that's Harumi peeking over the bowl).

GREEN SOUP

water cress

tofu cubes

green onions, diced

fresh sprouts

avocado pieces

garlic, fresh, chopped

cayenne

miso

Heat only, never boil. That way everything remains green and crisp.

Kathy served us this green soup with barbequed chicken and homemade bread.

JUNE KIRKWOOD
June Kirkwood had The Little Kitchen Restaurant for many years. She gives classes in how to cook with health foods.

LENTIL—BARLEY SOUP

This is a hearty one-dish meal. Use all organic ingredients where possible.

lentils — 2 cups

barley — ½ cup

carrots — 3

onions — 2

garlic — 3 cloves or to taste

basil or cumin powder — 1 teaspoon

miso/tamari or sea salt to taste

spring water

Wash lentils by covering with water, rubbing between hands. Pour off water. Do this three times. The last rinse may be done in a colander. Pick through for small stones or mud clumps.

Place in pressure cooker, cover three inches above lentils with spring water, add 1" piece of kimbula (a sea vegetable). Bring to pressure, lower flame to maintain pressure and cook for 45 minutes. If lentils are soaked overnight, 30 minutes will be sufficient time (or if at sea level).

If using sauce pan, soaking overnight will reduce cooking time, especially at high altitudes. 45 to 60 minutes should be sufficient.

Barley — proceed as for lentils, washing and rubbing three times. Cook in sauce pan 30 to 45 minutes in three times amount of water. Bring to boil and lower flame. Stir occasionally to avoid sticking.

Cut carrots, onion, and chop garlic and steam together in small amount of spring water, till tender. Longer cooking brings out natural sweetness of carrots and onions. Use soup kettle for this step.

When barley, lentils and vegetables are cooked...combine in Dutch oven or soup kettle. Season to taste with herbs and sea salt or tamari (soy sauce). If miso is used, dissolve desired quantity (start with ½ cup) in small amount of liquid before adding. For a salt-free diet, kelp may be used to replace salt, miso or tamari.

This should make 12-16 servings, depending on amount of spring water you may desire to add after the cooking is completed (to thin out or stretch).

A touch of lemon juice is a nice addition. This soup is wonderful on a cold day for lunch or dinner and great the next day (covered and refrigerated it will last for three to five days).

NORA FELLER
Nora is a portrait photographer; she works in Aspen, New York City and Paris and publishes in many national and international magazines.

CARROT SOUP WITH DILL

Yield: 6 servings

Ingredients:

2 tablespoons butter

¾ cup finely chopped onions

1 clove garlic, finely minced

1 ½ pounds carrots, scraped and sliced (about 4 cups)

4 cups fresh or canned chicken stock

salt and freshly ground pepper to taste

2 cups water

½ cup ricotta cheese

3 tablespoons port wine

2 tablespoons chopped fresh dill

Method:

1. Heat butter in a saucepan and add onions and garlic. Cook, stirring, until they are wilted. Add carrots, stock, salt, pepper and water. Bring to a boil and simmer for 20 minutes.

2. Strain over a saucepan to reserve the cooking liquid. Puree the solids in a food processor or food mill along with cheese and 1 cup of the reserved cooking liquid. Transfer the puree to the saucepan with the remaining cooking liquid. Blend well.

3. Bring soup to a boil and add wine and dill. Serve hot or cold.

THICK CREAMY ONION SOUP

Serves four people.

Slice four or five large white onions. Slowly saute in butter until golden yellow (not brown). Add six to seven cups of milk.

Simmer slowly for 20 minutes or more until onions are soft and sentimental. Add salt, pepper, small pinch of nutmeg and dash of garlic salt.

Place one slice of white toast in each soup bowl.

Sprinkle toast very generously with grated parmesan or romano cheese.

Pour hot soup over and eat!

FABI AND FRITZ BENEDICT

The Benedicts have been Aspenites since the 1940s. Fritz discovered the skiing when he was a member of the 10th Mountain Division (ski troopers) based over the mountain at Camp Hale. An architect, he has designed many of Aspen's homes and business buildings.

JILL SHEELEY

Jill has written another Aspen cookbook entitled "The Tastes of Aspen" which includes recipes from local restaurants. Here she is delivering a batch of books to Explore Book-Sellers.

BROCCOLI SOUP

Jill says this recipe originated as a cold zucchini soup and she changed it to a hot, hearty broccoli soup at the request of her family.

Ingredients:

3 tablespoons butter

1 bunch green onions, chopped

1¼ lb. broccoli (cut off bottom of the stalks and just use the flowers), cut into ½" pieces

6 cups chicken broth or stock

3 large potatoes, cubed

1½ teaspoon wine vinegar

¾ teaspoon dill weed

white pepper

4 tablespoons quick cooking farina

½ cup cooked barley (optional)

1 pint sour cream

Method:

Saute the onions in butter. Add the chicken stock, broccoli, potatoes, vinegar, and seasonings. Bring to a boil. Stir in farina and simmer partially covered for ½ hour.

In batches, place soup mixture in Cuisinart with 4 or 5 tablespoons of sour cream (until sour cream is used up). Place back on burner and reseason if necessary. If you like barley, add it at this point.

Note: This soup gets better each day. Jill serves it the second day along with hot, homemade bread or herb biscuits, a variety of cheese, and a large fresh vegetable salad.

A nice California Chardonnay wine complements this meal nicely.

LIVER SOUP

Make a soup stock by simmering for several hours about 3 quarts of water with a veal or beef soupbone, 3 stalks of celery, a carrot or two, an onion cut up. Drain the broth from the meat and vegetables, so you have a clear broth. Salt and pepper broth to taste.

Now:

¼ lb. liver, ground in meatgrinder
  2 slices onion, ground
      in meatgrinder
  1 egg
    salt and pepper to taste
    breadcrumbs
  1 teaspoon rind of lemon

Make all ingredients into medium hard paste. Let stand 5 minutes or more. With teaspoon drop little dumplings into boiling broth. Let simmer 10 minutes.

GRETL UHL
A former member of the German National Ski team . . .

She is as famous for her cooking at Gretl's Restaurant.

In rocky hideaway places the wild flowers grow.

MINESTRONE SOUP

 1 tomato, quartered
 2 lbs. meat (beef or veal) and knuckle or shank bones, cracked (the bones
   are what give the best flavor to the stock)
 3 quarts water
 1 medium sized onion, peeled and quartered
 1 carrot, quartered
  Handful of celery tops
 1 teaspoon salt
¼ teaspoon pepper
 2 cloves garlic
 4 strips bacon, cut up into small pieces
  Handful of endive or dandelion greens

1. Combine all ingredients into 4 quart kettle, cover tightly.

2. Bring to boiling — reduce heat — simmer 2 to 3 hours.

3. Remove bones and meat. Add ¼ lb. spaghetti, ¼ cup raw rice, 1 can kidney beans, 1 can green beans, ½ can corn (the latter two ingredients can also be frozen or fresh), parboiled potatoes, peas if desired. Dice boiled meat and add.

4. Cook mixture until spaghetti is done — 20 to 25 minutes.

5. The spaghetti and rice tend to thicken this soup — if necessary add a little more water. There is plenty of flavor and will not be ruined. Serve with cheese and crackers or croutons. A meal in itself.

CHERIE GERBAZ OATES
A teacher, former ski racer, and now married to an Attorney.

SAVORY AND EXOTIC CARROT SOUP TO LIVE FOR

Dice one large onion and saute in 2 tablespoons butter in saucepan.

Clean 2 lbs of carrots and shred them into a 4 quart saucepan.

Add 6 cups water

3 vegetable broth cubes

1 tablespoon fresh grated (peeled) ginger

¼ teaspoon cinnamon

¼ teaspoon ground cloves

2 tablespoons butter

salt and pepper to taste

Combine all ingredients in saucepan, bring to boil and simmer until done.

If carrots aren't sweet enough, you can add up to 4 tablespoons honey.

Garnish with a few slices of fresh carrot on top.

JOANIE KLAR

Joanie Klar is a leader in women's issues, she works for the betterment of the women and children of Indonesia, and women and children in the United States.

MEREDITH OGILBY lives in a magical Victorian house in the Crystal River Valley. She photographed women of the Roaring Fork Valley for her exhibit and her book both titled "A Life Well Rooted."

BUTTERNUT SQUASH SOUP

Serves 8

Ingredients

2 fairly large butternut squash

2 cups rich chicken broth (or maybe more)

1 small onion diced

2 tablespoons butter

2 tablespoons finely minced fresh ginger (1 tablespoon ground ginger may be substituted but fresh ginger makes all the difference)

½ to 1 cup heavy cream (half and half ok for lighter soup)

juice and rind of one lime

Method

1. Quarter squash, remove seeds and boil in a large pot filled with water until well cooked.

2. Remove squash from skin and mash or puree to desired consistency, add 1½ cups stock.

3. Saute onion in butter until translucent, add ginger and ½ cup stock. Simmer until very soft.

4. Puree onion and ginger mixture and add to squash mixture.

5. Cook the soup for about an hour adding more stock for a thinner soup.

6. Finish with cream and lime juice, just heating through. Garnish with grated lime rind.

CHRISTOPHER WALLING

Christopher Walling is an internationally known jewelry designer and he has a boutique in Aspen. His dog is "Jack."

AVOCADO VICHYSOISSE

a la Nancy MacDonald

½ cup light cream

1½ cups chicken broth or stock (1 can)

½ cup cold water

1 avocado (ripe and cut up)

1 clove garlic (cut up)

salt and pepper to taste

3 "squirts" of Tabasco

Blend all ingredients, except cream, for 15 minutes in a blender. Then add cream and blend for an extra 10 seconds. Serve chilled.

Christopher relates that Nancy MacDonald was a second mother to him, and wife of Dwight MacDonald, the literary figure. She devoted her fortune and life to the refugees of the Spanish Civil War.

Jackie Wogan took her pooch to pay a visit to Christopher Walling's boutique.

GREEN DRAGON CABBAGE AND NOODLE SOUP

¼ pound pork tenderloin

2 oz Szechuan preserved vegetable* (about ⅓ cup)

1 pound cabbage, cored, sliced ¾ inch thick and chopped (about half a medium cabbage, about 6 cups)

1 package ramen noodles, pork or Oriental flavor

½ teaspoon salt

2 teaspoons soy sauce

Slice pork tenderloin across the grain ¼ inch thick and cut slices into bite-size pieces. Arrange pork in a ring on a plate or dish, cover with a paper towel, and microwave at full power for one minute. The pork will not be fully cooked.

Slice Szechuan vegetable ⅛ inch thick and cut slices into dice. You should have about ⅓ cup.

Remove seasoning package from noodles and break noodles into manageable pieces (easily done inside original package).

Bring 4 cups water to a boil. Add noodles, cabbage, pork with its juices (breaking pieces apart), Szechuan vegetable, and salt. Stir. Bring back to a boil, reduce heat, cover, and simmer about 4 minutes, until noodles are done and cabbage is barely tender.

Remove from heat, add soy sauce and contents of seasoning package. Stir and serve.

*Szechuan preserved vegetable is widely available, canned or in plastic, in Oriental markets. It is an olive-green, rubbery tuber of irregular shape, about 3 inches in diameter, usually coated with hot spices which may be rinsed off.

Note: The reason for microwaving the pork is to prevent a scum from forming on the surface of the soup.

JANET GUTHRIE
INDIANAPOLIS MOTOR SPEEDWAY 1977

JANET GUTHRIE

Janet Guthrie is the first woman ever to compete in the Indianapolis 500. The year 2002 marked Janet's 25th anniversary at Indy, where she is the only woman to finish in the Top 10, as well as her 25th anniversary in the Daytona 500 NASCAR race, where she is the only woman ever to have qualified and competed. Photo is courtesy of Janet Guthrie.

WINTERSKOL

PATRICIA MOORE

You haven't been in Aspen
unless you've been to a
Patricia Moore Gallery Opening.

BUBA'S (GRANDMOTHER'S CHICKEN SOUP)

A rich, clear broth to be served with either matzoh balls, rice, kasha or fine noodles

one 3 to 5 lb. pullet or hen chicken	6 sprigs parsley
2 large ribs celery including tender leaves	2 medium sized carrots
1 large onion, ½ way quartered	1 medium sized marrow bone

Chicken may be cooked whole, quartered or in smaller pieces. (Include necks, feet, internal organs, except liver). Wash chicken in cold water, salt freely and let stand for ½-hour. Rinse salt off carefully.

Place chicken in heavy pot (with cover) with cold water to just cover (4 qts. or so). Bring to rapid boil and remove scum as it rises to surface. Continue to boil and skim for short period, until skum has been removed.

Turn heat very low, to simmer and continue to simmer with pot lid at angle for about an hour. Add seasoning, vegetables, continue to simmer another hour. Season to taste.

Cool and skim surface. Serve hot with matzoh balls.

MATZOH BALLS

1 cup matzoh meal	2 tablespoons rendered chicken fat (or butter)
2 eggs	salt, pepper to taste
½ cup water	¼ cup minced parsley may be used

Beat eggs lightly, add remaining ingredients and blend until smooth. Mixture should be loose but not runny. Refrigerate for at least ½ hour. After refrigeration, matzoh meal will have absorbed liquid so that it's possible to form balls which hold together. Size of balls may vary from walnut to extra large egg. Drop into rapidly boiling salted water and boil until tender, 20 minutes or so depending on size of matzoh balls. Drain in colander and serve with hot chicken broth.

PAT DASKO

The Aspen coordinator for Ballet West, Pat is much of the spirit and the work of bringing the ballet company to Aspen every summer.

POTAGE GARBAGE

First, get two large plastic bags, one is to save all raw vegetable parings and scraps, never letting yourself throw away anything again. The other bag is to save all bones, even the ones left on plates. All this is going into your freezer.

You'll find the veg bag gets filled first, so buy a beef knuckle or some chicken backs and you're ready to go.

Throw the bones into a nice sturdy pot with a tight cover. Cover with a good amount of water, add peppercorns, bay leaves, sprigs of anything nice in the herb family and about ¼ cup of vinegar. (White's nice but wine vinegar can be a surprise) and let the whole mess come to a bubble, covered for at least 3½ hours.

Good idea is to start in the AM, then come in after skiing and throw the bag of frozen vegetables in for about 20 minutes.

Let cool, strain and put into fridge to let fat rise up. Throw the vegetable and bone garbage out now.

Whenever fat has solidified, skim, put broth into large clean pot and you are ready to start the soup.

Use vegetables like zucchini, turnip, tomato, bean sprouts, carrots, celery, fresh parsley and ox tail or beef shanks or a stewing chicken with lots of dill, rosemary, bay leaves, garlic, pepper and a super dash of red or white wine depending on the strength of the meat.

Tastes better a day after and it is a hit for a supper when you want to invite a lot of friends but you are broke.

ELEANOR AND EVERETT BIGGS

Eleanor and Everett live in Aspen and in Knoxville, Tennessee. Eleanor is a landscape designer and Everett is just about the best cook you'll ever meet.

BLACK EYED PEAS AND CORNBREAD

    1 pound black eyed peas

Cover peas with water, two inches above, and soak overnight. Pour off water. Cover peas with fresh water in large kettle and add:

    large onion, chopped

    ½ teaspoon salt

    1 teaspoon sugar

    ¼ pound pork seasoned meat cut up into small pieces (not bacon)

Bring to a boil. Cut to simmer for four to six hours. Add water when needed.

Serve with Southern Cornbread

    1 cup corn meal (white preferred)

    1 cup plain flour

    ½ teaspoon salt (or to taste)

    1 teaspoon baking powder

    1 tablespoon sugar

Place in blender:

    ¼ cup milk

    2 eggs

    1 large cut-up onion

    1 medium green pepper

Blend above and pour over dry mixture. Before starting above, put 3 tablespoons of bacon drippings (or shortening) in 9" iron skillet. Place in 450 degree oven while mixing ingredients together. Pour half of drippings in batter, mix well. Pour in greased skillet, and bake in oven for approximately 40 minutes (high altitude) or when brown crust on top. 3 or 4 shakes of Vegit seasoning if desired.

Southern tradition says to serve black eyed peas on January 1. It brings good luck for the coming year.

MARY LOU TRENTAZ
Active in 4-H, Mary Lou can sew almost anything.

SCALLOPED CORN

1 can cream corn	2 teaspoons butter
1½ tablespoons cornmeal	3 tablespoons milk
¼ teaspoon salt	1 egg well beaten
2 teaspoons brown sugar	1½ tablespoons minced pimento

Combine corn, cornmeal, salt and brown sugar. Add butter, milk, egg and pimento. Bake in buttered casserole dish for 40 minutes at 325 degrees. Stir occasionally during first 20 minutes. Serves 4 or 5.

BAKED POTATOES
A LA ROARING FORK VALLEY

In the Fall of the year, many of us drive down the valley and buy our winter's supply of potatoes from ranchers.

Bake large potatoes and then cut lengthwise — take out insides of potatoes and set skins aside. Mash potatoes until fluffy with hot milk or cream and butter, salt and pepper. Put back into skins and sprinkle with either grated longhorn or parmesan cheese. Bake again until hot.

PIERENA USEL

The country around Basalt and Carbondale grows wondrous potatoes. It was at the Usel's ranch near Basalt where I first had potatoes fixed this way.

ANNIE DENVER

Annie Denver was the inspiration for "Annie's Song" written by John Denver.

PENNE WITH TOMATOES, OLIVES AND THREE CHEESES

6 to 8 servings, great for make ahead events and a crowd

6 tablespoons olive oil
1½ cups chopped onion
1 to 2 tablespoons chopped fresh garlic
3- 28 oz cans chopped plum tomatoes, drained
2 teaspoons dry basil
1 to 1½ teaspoons dried crushed red pepper flakes
2 cups canned chicken broth

1 pound penne
2½ cups packed grated cheese. Use a blend of mozarella, parmesan, jack
½ to ¾ cup pitted Kalamata olives
⅓ cup ground fresh parmesan
¼ cup finely chopped fresh basil

Heat 3 tablespoons olive oil in pan over medium high heat. Saute onion and garlic until transparent — about 5 minutes. Mix in drained tomatoes, dried basil, red pepper. Bring to boil, then add chicken stock, boil again. Reduce heat to medium and simmer to reduce mixture to a chunky sauce. (About 6 cups). Stir occasionaly, cook 1 hour and 15 minutes.

Preheat oven to 375 degrees. Cook pasta until tender, but still firm. Drain well, return to pot, and toss with remaining olive oil. Pour sauce over to blend. Mix in olives and cheese. Put in a 13x9x2 baking dish. Sprinkle with parmesan cheese. Bake until heated through — 30 minutes. Sprinkle with chopped fresh basil and serve. Delicious!

RANDY BEIER AND JANET O'GRADY

Randy and Janet, after years of working on **The New Mexico Magazine** and other regional magazines, came to Aspen and bought **Aspen Magazine**. Randy is publisher and Janet the editor of **Aspen Magazine**, which is not a travel guide, but a bona-fide city magazine.

This is one of their favorite Southwest recipes...a cuisine they learned to love after years of living in Santa Fe.

SOUTHWESTERN SUCCOTASH (serves four)

(This dish is sweet and hot — and colorful)

Shuck six heads of corn and cut the kernels off with a sharp knife, making sure no corn silks or pieces of corn cob are mixed into the kernels. Reserve the kernels while melting half a stick of sweet butter and ¼ cup olive oil in a high-sided saute pan over low heat. Dice coarsely, after de-seeding, one red bell pepper, and add to saute. Dice fine half a yellow onion and add to saute. Do not brown. When onion begins to turn translucent, add corn.

After the corn separates into individual pieces (3-5 minutes), add two minced poblano chiles (canned and ultra hot from Mexico), along with a splash of juice to taste — and tolerance Saute for another three minutes, until corn is hot through, but still crunchy and sweet. Add a squeeze of lime, a handful of minced cilantro, and serve.

Southwestern tiles.

DR. ARCHER AND SANDIE BISHOP

TOMATO PIE

Can make own crust or use Betty Crocker's Reabox pie crust.

Make pie crust in pie pan or quickie pan or shallow baking dish — may have to use several crusts. Pinch edges to decorate. Bake 10 minutes or about half the time called for.

When pie crust is slightly cooled, cut fresh ripe tomatoes in ½" slices-unpeeled. Layer in pan to top of edge of pan.

Sprinkle tomatoes with salt and pepper and fresh basil. Mix sharp grated cheddar-about three cups, with ¾ to 1 cup mayonnaise.

Use your hands and pat this mixture evenly over entire top, sealing edges of crust. Decorate top of cheese with bay leaves in center.

Bake at 400 degrees for 45 minutes.

Let sit 10 minutes.

Serve. Will be runny. Can use separate small bowls or plates.

Dr. Archer and Sandie Bishop have a beautiful ranch in the Owl Creek Valley where they enjoy riding their horses.

EXPLORE BOOKSELLERS AND BISTRO

Explore BookSellers and Bistro is one of those special book stores where you can cuddle down in an easy chair and read a good book...or have tea, luncheon or dinner by the fire or in the garden room.

BLANCA'S VEGGIE MEATLOAF

Serves 10

Recipe by Blanca Salas, Explore Bistro chef

    2 cups sliced mushrooms

    3 cups sliced yellow onions

    2 cups cooked organic brown rice

    3 cups cooked organic green lentils

    ⅓ cup firm tofu (about 3 ounces)

    1 cup organic ketchup

    ⅓ cup tamari soy sauce

    ½ cup Egg Replacer powder

    4 minced cloves garlic

    1 cup rolled oats

    ½ cup mashed potato flakes

    2 cups grated carrots

    1 tablespoon fresh thyme or ½ tablespoon dried thyme

    ½ tablespoon sea salt

    ½ tablespoon ground black pepper, to taste

Preheat oven to 350 degrees.

Spray a large saute pan with olive oil or canola oil. Cook onions and mushrooms over low heat until soft, about 12 minutes. Place mushrooms and onions in food processor. Add lentils, rice, ½ cup ketchup, tofu, garlic, and tamari, and process until smooth. Add Egg Replacer powder and 1 cup filtered water and process again. Place mixture in a bowl and add oats, carrots, potato flakes and thyme, mix well.

Line the bottom of a 9x5x3 loaf pan with parchment paper that has been cut to fit, with 2 inches extra on sides for easy removal after cooking. Oil the paper. Place mixture in the pan and spread evenly. Use a knife to make an "X" shaped groove in the top of the loaf, and spread remaining ½ ketchup over the top of the loaf. Cover tightly with foil

Bake in preheated oven until firm to the touch, about 2 hours

To unmold, first uncover, and allow the loaf to cool down for a few minutes. Lift meatloaf from pan by grasping the paper at both sides.

Slice and serve with gravy, mashed potatoes, and fresh green vegetables of your choice.

TERRY ANDERSON

Terry Anderson grew up in Hawaii and left the land of sunshine and the beach for the land of snow and skiing.

GREEN RICE

Serves 8 people

Cook 2 cups of regular rice (not sticky rice)

Let it cool some

Add:

2 beaten eggs

⅔ cup vegetable oil

2 cups grated cheddar cheese

Chop fine or put through cuisinart

2 onions

1 cup parsley (remove stems)

2 small green peppers

Mix all well and add

2 cups milk

Put in casserole

Sprinkle some cheese on top of casserole

Bake 350 degrees for 45 minutes

MARY JANE GARTH

Mary Jane Garth is famous for her picnics and parties at the picnic place on her Aspen Valley Ranch.

BAKED SWEET POTATOES AND APPLES

Serves six to eight

   6 medium sweet potatoes
½ cup milk
¼ cup butter
¼ cup honey
¼ cup orange juice
   1 medium apple, chopped finely
¼ cup chopped pecans
¼ cup raisins
marshmallows for topping

Cook, then peel sweet potatoes, then mash them with the milk and butter. Add chopped apple and rest of the ingredients, salt and pepper to taste, then stir well. Add mixture to well-greased 2 quart casserole.

Bake at 375 degrees for 35-40 minutes. Add marshmallows to the top and put under broiler until lightly browned.

Hans Rieger, left, plays the zither and Steen Gantzel plays the accordian at an Aspen summertime party.

MARIAN DAVIS

Marian Davis and her daughter, Tina Baar, at the Silver Baron Ball the year that Marian was crowned "The Silver Queen.

PECAN PRALINE SWEET POTATO CASSEROLE

Marian Lyeth Davis tells that this is a family recipe that has been handed down for several generations. Her family likes it so much that they have it for Thanksgiving, Christmas, and now for Marian's annual Blackeye-Pea party of January 1. It is a very Southern dish and Marian's family likes it lots with turkey or chicken.

2 cups mashed sweet potatoes, use canned because they are
  already cooked, drained quite well
2 cups cream
2 tbs melted butter
scant tsp salt
½ tsp cinnamon
¼ to ½ cup Bourbon

Topping
½ cup brown sugar
½ cup butter
1 cup pecan halves
scant tbs flour

Thoroughly mix potatoes, cream, melted butter, salt, cinnamon and Bourbon. Spread in greased casserole dish. Make the topping by heating the brown sugar and butter over low heat, stirring constantly until butter is melted. (It is important not to cook after butter is melted or topping will harden when casserole is baked). Spread topping over potatoes and cover with pecan halves. Refrigerate until ready to heat. Heat uncovered at 350 degrees for 30 to 35 minutes.

This recipe can be altered (for less fat) by using one egg and cutting down on the cream.

The Bowman Block in Aspen.

NANCY MAYER

Nancy Mayer is the Director of Sales and Associate Publisher of *Aspen Magazine*.

PARTY POTATOES

These potatoes are a favorite at every party: they can be breakfast, lunch or dinner potatoes for any occasion. Bake in a pretty casserole dish or use a throw away casserole dish and have no clean up at the end of the party.

Ingredients

1 bag plain, cubed, frozen Hash Browns (thaw before mixing)

1 can Campbell's condensed cream of chicken soup

1 16 oz container sour cream

1 cup shredded sharp cheddar cheese

1 cup shredded mild cheddar cheese

½ small onion finely chopped

1 stick butter

1½ to 2 cups crushed Cornflakes

salt and pepper to taste

Melt ⅓ stick butter in pan and slowly saute onions, set aside. In large bowl mix soup, sour cream and cheeses.

Next mix in the thawed potatoes, then stir in onions and butter and season to taste. Place mixture in casserole dish (spray with nonstick spray) and bake at 350 degrees for 40 minutes.

While potatoes are cooking, crush Cornflakes to have 1½ to 2 cups, set aside. Melt the other ⅔ of a stick of butter in a pan, when melted, mix in Cornflakes to coat with butter and set aside. After potatoes bake for 40 minutes, spread Cornflakes evenly over the top, place back in oven and continue cooking for 20 minutes. Remove from oven, serve and enjoy.

CONAN ANGELO

Conan is a trainer in a physical fitness gymnasium, he is a belly dancer, a country-western dancer, a rock singer, a cowboy at heart.

CONAN'S DIXIE DELIGHT

This dish is his favorite and was served to him by a sexy Southern Sweetheart and expert cook.

All raw vegetables used must be homegrown in Aspen. Any okra or black-eyed peas must be imported from Alabama (fresh is best).

Boil whatever proportions you want of whole okra and black-eyed peas till soft.

Serve with raw sliced peppers, onions, tomatoes and also with cornbread made with onions, hot peppers and buttermilk.

BIEGE AND GAIL JONES

Both Biege and Gail are bicycle racers. Biege is a graphic artist supreme, working many years for the **Aspen Times** and Sport Obermeyer. Gail works in marketing for Sport Obermeyer.

PASTA PRIMAVERA

4 tablespoons salt

½ pound egg fettuccine

½ pound mixed tomato and spinach fettuccine

1/3 cup olive oil

½ cup fine chopped purple onion

¾ pound snow peas

1/3 pound sugar snap peas

¾ pound prosciutto cut into thin slices

2 tomatoes, quartered

8 scallions, chopped

½ cup basil, fresh

fresh ground pepper to taste

4 tablespoons raspberry vinegar

¼ cup grated parmesan

1. Bring 4 quarts water to a boil. Add 2 tablespoons salt and stir in fettuccine. Cook until tender but still firm, and drain. Transfer to large bowl and add olive oil and chopped onion. Toss and set aside.

2. Bring another 4 quarts water to a boil. Add 2 tablespoons salt, snowpeas and sugar snap peas. Cook for 1 minute, drain and plunge peas into large bowl of cold water. Let stand for 10 minutes. Drain and pat dry.

3. Add peas to pasta along with prosciutto, tomatoes, scallions and basil. Season with salt and pepper, sprinkle on raspberry vinegar to taste and toss gently adding parmesan. 6 portions.

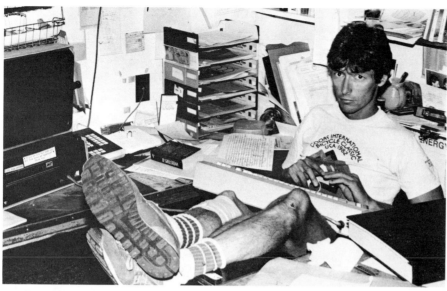

MICK IRELAND

Mick was a longtime reporter at the **Aspen Times**. Now he is an attorney and gets to harangue everyone in the courtroom instead of in the newspaper.

Mick's recipe is, of course, all in his own words.

I qualified for this latest edition of **Aspen Potpourri** because I am the director of the Aspen Times Five, a July 4 footrace that Mary Eshbaugh Hayes sometimes enters.

My alleged recipe is probably better classified as a low income, high energy eating style geared to maximize calorie assembly using minimum time and cost. I call it Brown Rice Surprise. The wonderful thing about brown rice, the real stuff, not instant rice with additives, is that one doesn't need to be precise about measuring or cooking the stuff nor need one worry about some doctoral candidate earning a good living off in a lab somewhere feeding rats the additives that make instant rice instant and consumers like myself a bit paranoid.

But I digress. Brown rice surprise requires only a cup of rice and twice as much water. The cup can be any size: left over Boulder Bolder Race cups, empty lemonade cans, beer mugs, pyrex beakers "borrowed" from a long-abandoned chemistry lab, even measuring cups have served this purpose well. Just remember to use twice as much water.

Bring water and rice to a rapid boil. That takes a while but again, precise measures are not necessary. Let's just say more time than an inning of televised baseball and less than one quarter of the typical NBA game. If the water is all gone, add more and start over. If the rice is either black, smoking or actually on fire, empty the pot and start again.

After you get a pot of water and unburnt rice boiling, turn the heat down to low and let it simmer until the rice absorbs all the water. While the rice is blotting up the water, go through the refrigerator for vegetables. The blotting process takes a half hour to an hour depending on altitude, attitude, water temperature and whether your utility bill is paid up for the near future. You'll definitely want to check when you get done sorting out the vegetables you want to use and throwing out those that have begun supporting life forms other than human.

Take the usable vegetables — I prefer green peppers and mushrooms — slice them into thin strips or small chunks and pan fry them with butter or margarine. Mix the two together and serve Brown Rice Surprise. I call it a surprise because it never comes out the same but always tastes surprisingly good. The left overs keep for weeks if properly refrigerated and brought back to life with sufficient megawattage of microwaves.

MARYANN GREENE

A knitter of beautiful ski sweaters, Mary Ann Greene often serves as an Ambassador for the Aspen Skiing Company.

VETEKRANS

This Swedish coffee bread is one of my son's favorites. I always make it when he comes home for a visit. Otherwise, it is traditionally baked for Christmas morning breakfast or when we have house guests.

Ingredients for Bread

1 tablespoon yeast
1 teaspoon sugar
¼ cup water (lukewarm)
4 oz sweet butter (1 stick)
⅓ cup sugar
1 tablespoon cardamom
½ teaspoon salt
¾ cup milk (scalded)
3¼ cup flour

Ingredients for Filling

8 oz almond paste
2 oz sweet butter
2 egg yolks (save whites and paint pastry before placing in oven)
½ cup confectioners sugar
8 oz sliced almonds
¼ cup cinnamon sugar (⅛ cup sugar and ⅛ cup cinnamon)

Procedure

1. In a small bowl, proof for 10 minutes: 1 tablespoon yeast, 1 teaspoon sugar, and ¼ cup water

2. In mixer bowl, place 4 oz of the butter, ⅓ cup sugar, 1 tablespoon cardamom, ½ teaspoon salt. Use paddle to mix ingredients.

3. Add ¾ cup milk, which was scalded in microwave or on top of stove in a small pan.

4. Let mixture cool. Then add yeast mixture to the butter mixture.

5. Gradually add in 3 cups of flour.

6. Knead, using dough hook, adding the remaining ¼ cup flour if necessary. Remember, the dough will form a ball and should feel smooth as a baby's bottom. This is an experience call. The dough should not be too dry or too wet.

7. Place dough into a buttered bowl and let rise until it has doubled in bulk. This first rising takes approximately 30 minutes at altitude.

8. Punch dough down and roll into a 10"x18" rectangle.

9. Spread with almond paste filling: In food processor, mix almond paste with the remaining 2 oz butter and ½ cup confectioners sugar. Add the 2 egg yolks and ½ cup sliced almonds. Save the rest for topping. Sprinkle with cinnamon sugar.

10. Roll dough up lengthwise and place on a buttered baking sheet.

11. With a pair of scissors, snip almost to the center in 1" intervals. Pull and turn until the piece lies flat forming a wreath or ring.

12. Let dough rise for 30 minutes in the ring until double.

13. Brush with egg white and sprinkle with the remaining ¼ cup of sliced almonds. Sprinkle with sugar.

14. Bake in a preheated 350 degree oven for 35 to 40 minutes.

Back in 1952, you just stuck your skis in the snowbank outside your hotel…and they were still there in the morning.

IOLA ILGEN

Head of a large family and known as one of the best cooks in the area.

CINNAMON ROLLS

At church and school bake sales, Mrs. Ilgen's cinnamon rolls are one of the first things snapped up.

Mix two yeast cakes in ¼ cup lukewarm water and one tablespoon sugar — let set until it is working good.

1 pint milk scalded and then cooled
1 teaspoon salt

3 eggs
⅔ cup sugar
¼ lb. butter

Mix together well the eggs, salt, sugar and butter — then add cooled milk and yeast and enough flour to make a stiff dough. Let raise until double in bulk. Melt ¼ lb. butter, roll dough ¼" thick, spread with butter, cinnamon and brown sugar, cut in strips and roll. Sometimes add the juice and rind of one lemon to the dough for a variation in flavor. This dough can be kept in refrigerator. Bake in moderate oven. Makes about 3 dozen.

SPONGE

Some people do better with rolls and breads if they start with a sponge — so Mrs. Ilgen tells how she makes hers. Take your yeast (mixed with water), tablespoon of sugar, milk and a little flour to make a little stiffer consistency than cake dough — let this raise and then add the rest of ingredients of whatever recipe.

BANANA BREAD

3 very ripe bananas	1 egg
¾ cup sugar	1 teaspoon soda
pinch of salt	1 tablespoon water
¼ cup butter	2 cups pastry flour

Mash bananas with a fork. Blend in sugar, salt, and beaten egg. Melt butter and stir into banana mixture. Dissolve soda in water and add with sifted flour. Mix and bake in loaf pan for 45 minutes in 350 degree oven. Makes 1 loaf.

Note: Molasses and nuts may be added if desired. At high altitude a longer baking period is required.

BILLIE ERICKSON
Tennis player and lady airplane pilot.

Hallam Lake

BONNIE BRUCKER

Teaches modern dance — and on a trip to Denmark with husband Hans, Bonnie learned how to make

DANISH PASTRIES (Wienerbrod)

Basic Dough

1 cup cold milk	2 cups margarine
2 oz. yeast	5 cups flour or slightly less
¼ cup sugar	1 egg for brushing
2 eggs	½ cup flour to roll dough in

In large mixing bowl work the yeast, sugar and eggs with the fingers into the milk, then sift in 2 cups of flour and mix until smooth. Add the rest of the flour (sifted) to form a dough which can be kneaded. Knead on floured surface until you have a dough that slides smoothly in the hands. Roll dough into large rectangle ½" thick. Spread ⅔ cup of margarine thinly over ⅔ section of the rectangle. Fold inwards the **unbuttered** third from one end and another **buttered** third from the other end over on top of the first so that the dough is in 3 layers. Roll out the dough again to a ½" thick rectangle and repeat this process with another ⅔ cup margarine. Repeat once more in exactly the same way, making a total of 3 roll outs. Set to cool for 15 minutes. You now have enough dough for about 30 pastries — 3 different varieties. Here are some you might like to try.

I. SPANNDANERS

⅓ Wienerbrod dough   chopped nuts

    raspberry jam or vanilla custard   sugar icing

    Roll ⅓ dough into rectangle 20″ long by 6″ wide. Cut lengthways into 2 strips. Cut each strip into 5 equal parts, thus forming a total of 10 squares of dough. Fold in the 4 corners of each towards the center and press down well. Place on baking sheet with plenty of space between each. Brush with beaten egg. Place a dot of raspberry jam or vanilla custard in the middle of each and sprinkle with chopped nuts. Set aside to raise for 15 minutes. Bake at 350 degrees for 15 minutes. When cold spread sugar icing on each.

II. TRIANGLES

⅓ Wienerbrod dough   chopped nuts

    vanilla custard   egg for brushing

     sugar icing

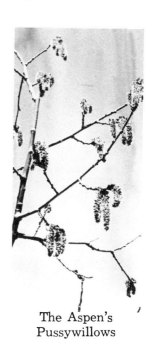

Roll out dough and cut into 10 squares — as for Spanndaners. Put a dot of vanilla custard (or what I do is mix vanilla custard with cream cheese and sugar to give a cheese filling) in the center of each square and fold over forming a triangle. Press the edges well together and make about 5-6 slashes in each edge with a knife, remembering not to cut clear to the center where the filling is. Brush with beaten egg and sprinkle a few chopped nuts in the middle. Place on baking sheet and raise for 15 minutes — bake at 350 degrees for 15 minutes and ice.

The Aspen's
Pussywillows

III. DINNER ROLLS

⅓ Wienerbrod dough   eggs for brushing

     sesame or poppy seeds

    Roll ⅓ of dough into a circle and cut into pie shaped wedges. Roll each section inward and place point side down on a baking sheet. Brush with beaten egg and sesame or poppy seeds, raise and bake.

    A tip that applies to all variations of Wienerbrod — eat them as oven fresh as possible — for they are never meant to be kept in a tin. I usually make the dough the day before and refrigerate it overnight — the pastries are then made the next morning and are ready for the breakfast table.

DIANA KOSMAN
A student and teacher of Art — Diana likes to bake bread.

A VERY GRAINY ANADAMA BREAD

1 tablespoon active dry yeast (or
    one package compressed
2 cups warm water
¼ cup oil or butter
¼ cup blackstrap molasses
¼ cup honey
3 teaspoons salt
⅓ cup rye meal

½ cup coarse yellow corn meal
    soaked in 1 cup water for about
    an hour
1 cup wheat germ
3 cups of whole wheat flour with a
    little rye flour
approximately 2 cups unbleached
    white flour

Put the yeast in warm water in a fairly large bowl and let dissolve. Add the oil, molasses, honey, salt and cornmeal mixture. Mix well and add the rye meal and wheat germ first in order to absorb the liquid. Next, add the flours one cup at a time, beating well until stiff. When the dough is too heavy to beat with a spoon, you are ready to knead on a floured board. Knead until firm, smooth and elastic. Place in a large well greased bowl. Turn the dough over and cover with a clean dry cloth. Place in a warm or sunny window and let raise until doubled. Punch down and let the dough rest while you grease the pans. Shape into loaves, place in bread pans and bake at 400 degrees for 20 minutes and 350 degrees for 50 minutes. For small loaves less time is needed and wide loaves tend to need more time. Cool right side up on a rack.

80

DAVID AND BRIDGET KERR

Own the Hutch, a shop for young Victorians.

CARROT BREAD

¾ cup cooking oil
1 cup sugar
2 eggs
1½ cup sifted flour
1 teaspoon cinnamon
1 teaspoon soda
½ teaspoon salt
1½ cup finely grated raw carrots
¼ cup nuts

Combine oil and sugar. Add eggs. Beat. Combine all dry ingredients. Add egg mixture and stir well. Fold in carrots and nuts. Pour into greased loaf pan or three little loaf pans. Bake at 350 degrees for one hour.

Along Glidden's Hill.

Hiking up the Difficult Creek Trail.

Looking over Montezuma Basin.

MADELEINE OSBERGER AND JANE WILSON

Reporters for the **Aspen Times**, Madeleine (left), who is a ski racer herself, is the ski editor. Jane (right), who lives in Carbondale, is the downvalley editor.

JANE'S PUMPKIN BREAD

3 cups sugar	3 1/3 cups flour
½ teaspoon baking powder	1 cup Crisco or shortening
2 teaspoons baking soda	1 cup water
1 teaspoon cloves	15-oz. can pumpkin
1 teaspoon cinnamon	1 cup nuts
1½ teaspoon salt	

Combine all but nuts...mix well, then add nuts. Put in greased pans. Makes two regular loaves or four small loaves. Bake at 325 degrees for 1½ hours for regular loaves, small loaves for 50-55 minutes.

MADELEINE'S ZUCCHINI BREAD

3 eggs	1 teaspoon baking soda
2½ cups sugar	¼ teaspoon baking powder
1 cup oil	2 cups grated zucchini (unpeeled)
1½ teaspoons vanilla	3 cups sifted flour
3 teaspoons cinnamon	1 cup chopped nuts
1 teaspoon salt	

Beat eggs until foamy in mixing bowl. Add sugar, oil, vanilla, cinnamon, salt, soda, baking powder, zucchini, and flour. Mix well. Turn batter into two 9x5 inch loaf pans and bake at 350 degrees for 1 hour and 20 minutes or until done when you put toothpick in center and it comes out clear. Remove from pan and cool on rack.

MARGE BABCOCK AND NORMA DOLLE

Twins Marge and Norma have twin Victorian lodges next door to each other on Cooper Avenue in Aspen. Marge has the Little Red Ski Haus and Norma has The Snow Queen. Marge and Norma also appeared in the "Which Twin Has the Toni" advertisements during the 1950s.

MARGE'S COFFEE CAKE

Mix three cups of flour, two cups of sugar, a cup of pecan and almond nuts, a cup of butter, a cup of cherries and a can of condensed milk. Add desired flavoring. Bake one hour and 10 minutes in oven at 350 degrees. Marge says this is easy and a favorite to serve at The Ski Haus.

NORMA'S BREAKFAST CRUMB CAKE

Set oven at 350 degrees. Grease and flour 8" square pan.

¼ cup butter

3-ounce package cream cheese

¾ cup sugar

1 egg

1 cup flour

1 teaspoon baking powder

¼ teaspoon baking soda

½ cup milk

½ teaspoon vanilla

¼ teaspoon almond extract

Cream butter and cream cheese, add sugar and cream, add egg and mix well. Sift dry ingredients. Add alternately with milk. Mix all. Spread in greased and floured pan.

Put topping on: ¼ cup flour, ¼ cup sugar, ¼ cup butter. Cut in for crumb mixture. Add ¼ cup chopped pecans. Bake 35 to 40 minutes.

MARGE'S GLUHWEIN RECIPE

Marge serves this gluhwein after skiing at the Little Red Ski Haus.

1 gallon Paisano or Vino Fino wine

1 cup sugar

3 cups water

1 box raisins

1 apple (cored and pared and chopped up)

1 lemon, sliced

1 orange, sliced

3 cinnamon sticks

6 cloves

Add water to wine, then sugar. Add all other ingredients and simmer for about 10 minutes when it is ready to serve. Depending on how sweet people like this gluhwein, more or less sugar can be added. Also water can be less if desired.

Little Red Ski House

Snow Queen Lodge

TED CONOVER

Ted is an author of non-fiction...notably
Coyotes and Rolling Nowhere.

BRING BACK CINNAMON TOAST

In this age of breakfast burritos, Egg McMuffins, five-grain breads and fancy bagels, Ted says it's important not to let our breakfast heritage slip away.

Use these ingredients:

ground cinnamon

sugar

butter

toast

Avoid "raw" sugar, brown sugar, or any sugar other than regular, old, white, refined, sugar bowl sugar. (Do not substitute honey.)

Plain white bread is the best, as other fancier, more "nutritious" breads, like fancy sugars, tend to have their own flavors, which obscure the cinnamon.

Avoid butter substitutes, as they are an affront to good taste.

Mix the cinnamon and sugar together in a big old salt shaker. More cinnamon than sugar. Shake on heavily buttered toast. Beware of using too little! (Remember how your mom used to do it...that way's best.) Savor.

ROCKY MOUNTAIN POPPY SEED FRUIT BREAD

Need four bread loaf pans. Grease and flour sides and bottom.

Ingredients:

1 box pre-mixed banana bread

1 box pre-mixed pumpkin bread

4 cooked prunes

4 cooked plums

2 cooked peaches

¼ cup canned pumpkin

¼ cup applesauce

6 dates (seeded)

1 ripe banana

2 eggs

½ teaspoon cinnamon

¼ cup butter (melted)

¼ cup sugar

¼ cup poppy seed

Take all the fruit and puree together. Mix in eggs, butter, sugar and cinnamon and poppy seeds. Mix all with boxes of pre-mixed banana and pumpkin bread.

Pour all ingredients into 4 loaf pans.

Cook at 350 degrees until firm.

Serve with breakfast, lunch or dinner.

KATHERINE FARISH RIVERS
Kate is an Aspen entrepreneur. Among her small businesses have been Ma Kate's Pies and Katherine's Baskets.

THE ASPEN SKI CLUB
50th Anniversary, December 1987

Members of the 10th Mountain Ski Troops who came back for the 50th Anniversary of the Aspen Ski Club were: (left to right) George Loudis, Ralph Ball, John Tripp, and Jose Acebo.

Aspen Ski Club racers in 1952 are: (front row) Wes Thorpe, Gale (Spider) Spence, and Dorothy Helmkamp. Back row (left to right): Max Marolt, Ted Armstrong, Tom Weld, and Bud Marolt.

Andre Roch planned and helped cut the original Roch Run for the Aspen Ski Club back in the 1940s. He came back to Aspen from Europe for the Ski Club's 50th Anniversary. Left to right are Andre Roch and Werner Kuster, longtime owner of The Red Onion.

RUTH WHYTE

Ruth Whyte was a tireless worker with the Aspen Ski Club for many years; now she is a tireless volunteer with the Aspen Historical Society. She has been the force behind many of the "anniversary" celebrations held in recent years. These anniversaries include the 40th Anniversary of the Aspen Skiing Company, the 50th Anniversary of the Aspen Ski Club, the 100th Anniversary of the Hotel Jerome, and the 100th Anniversary of the Wheeler/Stallard House which is the museum for the Historical Society. In this photo Ruth dances at the Ski Club anniversary with John Wilcox, owner of the Ashcroft cross-country ski area.

RHUBARB BREAD

Makes two loaves.

In an electric mixer bowl, combine: 3 eggs, 1 cup salad oil, 1¾ cup firmly packed brown sugar, and 2 teaspoons vanilla. Beat until thick and foamy. Stir in 2½ cups finely diced and washed rhubarb and ½ cup chopped walnuts.

In a separate bowl combine: 1½ cup each of...all purpose flour and whole wheat flour that is unsifted. 1½ teaspoons soda (2 teaspoons in low altitude), 2 teaspoons ground cinnamon, 1 teaspoon salt, and ½ teaspoon each of...baking powder, ground nutmeg, and allspice.

Add to rhubarb mixture and stir gently until blended. Bake in 2 greased 9x5 loaf pans at 350 degrees for 1 hour or until wooden pic inserted in center comes out clean. Turn out on a wire rack to cool.

JACK ROBERTS

An artist who paints pictures of the Old West, Jack Roberts lives and works in a studio in Redstone. Jack worked as a cowboy in his youth, so his paintings tell it like it really was. He shows Bates some of his sketches.

SOURDOUGH PANCAKES

Jack says this is the sourdough recipe he used as a cowboy years ago. All of the ingredients are to be found in any cowcamp. No perishables are used.

Sourdough starter: Boil some potatoes and save the potato water. Use 2 cups lukewarm potato water with enough flour to make a thick dough. Put this mixture into a crock, cover and set it in a warm place to ferment for a few days.

To make flapjack batter: Note: Always make more flapjack batter than you need so you can return leftover batter to the starter in the crock. Return to the starter crock as much batter as you removed. If very little batter is left, make up the difference with flour and canned evaporated milk. Mix leftover batter gently, by hand, into remaining starter in crock and return it to a warm place.

Mix:
1 cup sourdough starter
1 cup flour
2 tablespoons bacon grease
¼ cup canned evaporated milk

Blend in:
1 teaspoon baking soda
2 tablespoons sugar
pinch of salt

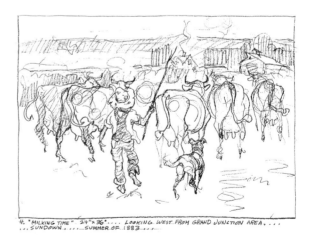

4. "MILKING TIME" 24"x 36".... LOOKING WEST FROM GRAND JUNCTION AREA....
... SUNDOWN .... SUMMER OF 1883 ...

Let mixture bubble a minute and then drop by spoonfuls onto hot griddle. Warm the syrup, boil up a big pot of coffee, and invite the neighbors in!

Recipe reprinted courtesy of Leanin' Tree of Boulder, Colorado, which originally printed the recipe, with Jack's painting of an old cowboy, as a Christmas card.

KIKI CUTTER

Kiki Cutter is a 1968 Olympic skier and a five-time World Cup ski champion. Every year she hosts a Spirit of Skiing weekend in Aspen during which she honors former and current stars of the skiing world.

KIKI CUTTER'S FAMOUS PANCAKE RECIPE

    1 egg
1¼ cup buttermilk.
       Kiki uses more buttermilk
       based on consistency.
       She likes the batter thinner.
    2 tablespoons soft shortening
1¼   sifted Gold Medal flour

Beat in:
    1 tsp sugar
    1 tsp baking powder
   ½ tsp baking soda
   ½ tsp salt

Better if left in refrigerator overnight.

SWEDISH PANCAKES
A LA DOROTHY THAU

Traditional

    1 cup sifted flour
    ½ teaspoon salt
    2 tablspoons sugar
    1 teaspoon vanilla
    1½ eggs
    2 cups milk
    ½ stick butter, melted

Mix flour, salt and sugar. Beat eggs and combine with milk. Gradually add flour mixture, beating until smooth. Slowly pour in melted butter. Heat skillet or griddle until hot. Pour on batter to desired pancake size. Flip over when bubbly. Pancakes should be golden brown on each side. Serve with powdered sugar, fresh raspberries, jam, etc.

Low-Fat Version

Substitute eggbeaters for eggs; use non-fat milk and canola oil.

DOROTHY THAU

Hal and Dorothy Thau dance at the Aspen/Santa Fe Ballet Summer Sizzler.

The Grottos are on Independence Pass and are giant caves carved by rocks and ice.

JEAN KNIGHT

She has a knack for turning out wonders with her sewing machine and some little imagination.

CIRCLE HAT — or SPRING FACE SAVER

Ingredients

Two 26" circles, any material   wide bias tape   elastic

Cut two circles of material. Jean cuts around her pizza pan as it is just the right size. Sew together on wrong side — leave small opening to turn to right side. Iron, turning under raw edge of opening and handstitch. Measure 3 inches in from outside edge of circle — sew bias tape around circle 3 inches in-all the way around. Run thin elastic under tape to fit head and hand finish ends of tape and elastic. Decorate to taste.

Notes: A 2 inch brim is more becoming, but a 3 inch brim makes a better sun hat. You can also vary the size of the circle to make your hat more or less floppy. Pauli Hayes wears a hat she made from this recipe on page 112.

ELLI HAYES
In a scarf made from print hanky.

HANKY HEADSCARF

The handmade hankies that you can buy in many of the Aspen shops are just too pretty to blow your nose on — and also hate to tuck them away in dresser drawers.

Elli discovered a perfect use — fold the hanky into a triangle, sew 10" long bias strips to each side — wear as headscarf.

A lace hanky
makes a Sunday scarf.

TO REFINISH FURNITURE

Wood can be a living, warm part of your household. Many unwanted pieces of furniture have been made useful again by refinishing the surface. Provided the basic design and quality of wood are sound, you can gain much enjoyment and accomplishment with this venture.

Ingredients

Ample space to work
paint remover
coarse steel wool
fine steel wool (00)
water (prepare for water runoff)
coarse sandpaper
very fine sandpaper
a good flat varnish
brushes, turpentine
lots of elbow grease

Pace yourself when refinishing any object. Do not expect to do it in a day, but plan to take as long as it takes to do a good job.

Remove the old surface — put paint remover on and leave long enough to bubble, work with coarse steel wool and wash off, repeat the process till most is off. Now remove the stubborn spots with coarse sandpaper — watch the edges and any fine work on the wood. Coarse sandpaper and a heavy hand will do damage. Sanding machines, too, are tricky and I prefer to do it all by hand. After working the wood with the coarse sandpaper, go over it with the fine sandpaper, rubbing it as you go with your hand to test smoothness. Rub now with the fine steel wool.

Put object in bright sunlight, wash with pure water repeatedly until grain has all been raised up. Let dry thoroughly. Mix 3 parts turpentine to 1 part varnish (I prefer a dull flat varnish) and apply to seal the pores. Let dry and rub with the fine steel wool. Apply another coat of the varnish mixture, let dry and rub with fine steel wool — repeat until you have the patina which you desire.

Wax with a mixture of ⅓ mineral oil, ⅓ turpentine and ⅓ linseed oil.

JOYCE GOULD
An admirer and
collector of
beautiful things.

ARIEL MURRI
Feeding Cricket, her cowbird.

RECIPE FOR REARING ORPHANED ROBINS, SPARROWS, COWBIRDS, BLUEBIRDS, ETC., TO MATURITY

To be made fresh each day: ¼ cup Pablum — mix with water to make a thin gruel to use with eyedropper. (Pointed glass eyedropper works better than blunt plastic ones.)

For older fledglings (those with full feather growth), a small amount of ground beef or canned dog food should be added to Pablum mixture. The mixture should be thicker though still liquid enough to use with eyedropper.

Method: The first feeding is usually a forced one. Gently pry open the bill and put eyedropper fairly far in the back of the throat before releasing food from eyedropper. Most young birds readily come to recognize the source of food and will open their mouths if lightly touched on the bill with the eyedropper. Feed as much as will be accepted each time. This must be at least every 45 minutes throughout the day for naked fledglings for the first week. Four or six feedings a day are not sufficient to keep young birds alive. Older fledglings must still be fed frequently — no less than eight times a day.

A small deep cardboard box will serve best as a safe and protected place to keep a very young bird even if a cage is available. A nest made from kleenex will make it easy to keep the box clean and comfortable. For naked birds, a 15 watt light bulb will keep them warm until feathers grow.

HENRY PEDERSEN

Landscape artist — Hank was a member of the Danish Gymnastic Team.

TRANSPLANTING IN ASPEN

To have better luck in transplanting trees or shrubs, bring them down from a higher elevation to a lower, or from a poor soil condition to a good soil condition. Aspen trees do excellently if brought down from a higher altitude. Prune back to make a balance between the root system and the foliage, because you lose an important amount of feeder roots by transplanting.

You should only transplant in the Spring before the leaves have budded or in the Fall after through leafing. Most important is good soaking with water for the first couple of years.

JEAN BAINBRIDGE

In a window she designed "to let the outdoors in." A ski instructor in winter, Jean decorates houses in summer — she has 14 houses to her credit and 2 ski lodges — mostly in the Santa Fe and Aspen areas. Below are some of her decorating tips, which she calls

CREATIVE HOUSEKEEPING

In this country of views — let the light, air, sunshine and view in. Use lots of windows — but not fuddy duddy dusty curtains.

Several fireplaces are especially good in a cold climate with a long winter — have one in your bedroom.

Bring things in from outdoors to help you through the long winters — weeds, roots, stones, pine boughs, red scrub oak boughs. Place them throughout the house.

Jean designed a "greenhouse window" for a house on Buttermilk —

when she got something to bloom, she moved it into the rooms for color —
when it finished blooming, put it back in the window.

Keep alive possibilities of things you own. An ancient ice box that once
held garden tools is now the Hi Fi cabinet. An old pine bed came in to be a
second sofa for the living room — smothered with pillows. A horse collar
could be hung over the kitchen fireplace — put flowers in it.

Walk-in closets with lots of shelves — so clutter can be easily stored
away and easily found again.

Live with something before you decide what to do with it.

White walls give you more leeway with design.

Don't take convenience over beauty — have a sunken living room, a
candelabra over the dining area, couple of steps up or down, those extra
fireplaces.

POTPOURRI

Use the wild pink roses which bloom in the Rockies in late June, the yellow roses which bloom in Aspen in early July — or a mixture of wild flowers. I always include some rosebuds whole — but as tiny as possible.

Pick the petals of flowers in the early morning, toss lightly on waxed paper in a cool, airy place to dry. Sprinkle with salt. Allow to stand 10 days stirring daily. Then put in your Potpourri jar. New petals can be added until jar is full.

Recipe which follows is for two quarts.

1 tablespoon Mace

2 tablespoons allspice

2 tablespoons cloves

2 tablespoons stick cinnamon broken in bits

2 tablespoons nutmeg

4 tablespoons powdered Orris root

1 tablespoon dried orange peel

Mix these ingredients together, then add to dried flower petals — a layer of spices, a layer of petals, a layer of spices — on up to the top of the jar. Keep in large bottles for looks or decanter into small bottles with holes punched in lid to let out aroma. Keep in dresser draws for a breath of summer.

MARY ESHBAUGH HAYES
With her children, gathering wild flowers for potpourri. Writer of "Around Aspen" for *The Aspen Times*.

LYNNE WILLE
She has bouquets of wild flowers framed in her kitchen — this is
how she dried them.

FLOWER-DRY

For drying flowers without losing color. The borax draws the moisture
from the flower more quickly — and the cornmeal keeps the flower from becoming too brittle.

Mix 1 cup borax with 5 cups corn meal. (This can be used over and over.)

Lay newspapers on flat board. Cover them with soft cloth such as old
sheeting. Arrange freshly picked flowers. Sprinkle with flower-dry. Cover with
soft cloth, pane of glass (or board) and weights. Flowers will be dry in a week.

At the Harrell-Pennario concert at the Opera House are, left to right: Cellist Lynn Harrell, film and TV star Robert Wagner, film and TV star Don Johnson, pianist Leonard Pennario. and film actress and cookbook author Jill St. John.

Backstage at the Wheeler after their Christmas concert are bass player Ben Wolfe, drummer Shannon Powell, and Jazz pianist supreme Harry Connick Jr.

Playing Concert

Glenn Yarbrough and the Hard Travelers came back to the Wheeler for a nostalgic evening of folk singing. Left to right are: Mike Munford and Buddy Renfro in back, then Mack Bailey with Glenn Yarbrough (Glenn in center with white beard), Ken Roberts and Mike Ritter.

MERRI JESS HAYES (Bates)

Bates sews on her patchwork quilt.
The recipe came from her great-grandmother.

PATCHWORK QUILT

Cut material in 4″ x 4″ squares.

The basic block is of four of the 4″ squares.

Pick two squares of matching patterns, sew one to an opposite pattern, and then again to the opposite . . . to form the basic block (as pictured).

When you get a whole lot of blocks made, sew them together in long strips. Then sew the strips together.

Decide how big you want the quilt and make the backing. Bates wanted her quilt to be 80″ x 72″. She found quilted red calico 40″ wide. She bought 4 yds. (144″) of the calico which she cut in half and then sewed together to make a backing of 80″ x 72″.

On the floor lay down the backing and fit patchwork (all sewn together) over the top until they match.

Once the top matches the bottom, turn under the raw edges and baste the back to the front. Then sew the seams on the sewing machine.

To finish, tie yarn through at the corners of the blocks.

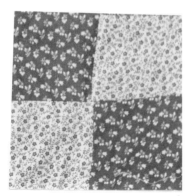

The basic block.

Put the blocks together and you have a quilt.

MOUSE TRAP

As Tony says, you never seem to have a trap in the house when you hear a mouse scratching about. So here is the recipe for one he makes.

Make about 4 cuts across top of plastic cover of 3 lb. coffee can. Place piece of cheese in center. Make staircase of books for mouse to climb up. When you hear him clattering around in the can, you have caught the mouse, and can take him outside and turn him loose.

TONY KASTELIC

A marvelous carpenter — here Tony and his "assistant" Merri-Jess begin work on our staircase.

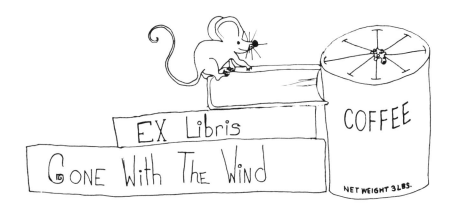

GERALD B. DE FRIES

Former principal of Aspen Middle School, Jerry now works with Outward
Bound and Outdoor Education.

OUTDOOR CAMPING HINTS

When planning a mountain hike or expedition, certain cautions and arrangements can insure a beautiful and rewarding experience.

1. Essentials for mountain traveling — map (obtain from Forest Service or
U.S. Geological Service), compass, flashlight (spare batteries), sun glasses,
spare food, extra clothing (sweater, jacket, rain parka or poncho, wool cap,
socks), matches, candle, pocket knife, first aid kit, whistle. Take along those
other supplies such as sleeping bag that you feel you need depending on
length of stay.

2. Make sure your boots are broken in, or worn and fit prior to your all-day
or overnight outing.

3. Have at least three people in your group, and set a slow, deliberate, rhyth-
mic pace. The pace of the group is the pace of the slowest person.

4. It is vital that a group stay together in the mountains.

5. Maintain a time control. Estimate the time to your destination, and the expected return. It has been offered by some that you should allow 1 hour for every 2 miles. You can probably move faster than this, but it allows time to roll in the meadow grasses and sniff the wild flowers. Descend in one-third of that time.

6. Maintain climate control for yourself — don't get too hot. Adjust clothing by opening collar or removing sweater, then put them on again as needed.

7. Be on the lookout for changing weather conditions, particularly clouds bearing lightning. If caught on a summit or pass, or ridge during a storm, move quickly to lower altitude and sit out the storm in a squatting position.

8. Use your map often to determine your location, check your hike-plan, and learn about the terrain.

9. If you build any fires, make sure your fire is completely out and the ashes scattered before you leave the campsite.

Skiing at Buttermilk.

TAGE PEDERSEN

Director of the Health Center at the Aspen Institute for
Humanistic Studies.

KEEPING FIT

To get in shape for skiing and to stay in
shape for living, Tage has found that rope
skipping is an excellent conditioner. It can be
done by anyone, anywhere and it is fun to do.
Start out easy — one minute a day for a week,
then try to add a minute a day per week.

Research has found that 10 minutes of
rope skipping is equivalent to 30 minutes of
jogging as a workout for your heart and
lungs (circulatory-respiratory system). Also it
strengthens your legs, improves coordination
and general fitness.

Tage rope skipping at the Health
Center.

ANNIE'S ART

The discovery of a water sculptured knurl of wood, a clump of interesting dried weeds, bright fabric scraps, or a weathered slab of barnwood ignites the creative in Annie.

Fondling the piece until she can feel the potential of beauty within and then rendering a decorative or useful item from "mere nothing" is a most exciting challenge. Hobby kits and bolts of new material simply stultify.

Whimsically recreating nature's work, the fragile woodland mushroom can become a carved-wood wall plaque or a grouping of paisley toadstools on burlap. Appliqueing bold flowers, fat little birds, or twining leaves on little girl's jumpers, curtains, bedspreads, even long hostess skirts makes them bloom with originality.

ANNIE CARTER

Carving a wooden mushroom at her kitchen workbench.

HILDA THURSTON

Outdoor enthusiast Hilda bicycles every day from her home up Independence Pass to the Library where she works.

Summer skiing at Montezuma Basin

TRAIL FOOD

Grind together into large bowl

2 cups prunes	1 cup pecans
1 cup dates	2 cups raisins
1 cup coconut	1 cup dried apricots
1 cup walnuts	1 cup toasted wheat germ

½ cup peanuts (optional)

Knead until well blended. Run through grinder again with 2 teaspoons of Rose Hip concentrate. Divide into 6 parts. Roll each to 1½ inches diameter, then roll in fine coconut. Wrap in wax paper, put in plastic bag and chill. Slice for serving or break off pieces when hiking or biking, or skiing.

SWEET PICKLE CHIPS

7 lbs. medium cucumbers cut in ½-inch slices. 2 cups canning salt to 1 gallon water. Soak cukes in brine for 5 days in large crock or plastic bucket. Keep chips under water with weight on plate. Stir daily. Drain, soak for 2 days in clear water. Drain and cover with clear boiling water in which 2 tablespoons alum has been dissolved (be sure to be accurate in measuring alum). Let stand 24 hours, drain and cover with clear boiling water — let stand till cool. Drain.

Syrup

6 lbs. granulated sugar

3 pints vinegar

4 teaspoons whole mixed spices

4 teaspoons celery seed

Bring syrup to a boil and pour over pickles. Let stand 24 hours. Drain syrup and reheat and pour over pickles again. Put pickles in jars and add reheated syrup. Can keep in crock or jars.

SHADY LANE

A 10th Mountain Division member who settled in Aspen after the war.

The Jerome Pool fence.

113

SANDY PELLETIER

Skiing at Buttermilk with her children. Since Monique doesn't show (she's in the pack on Sandy's back), see her below in her lederhausen.

HOW TO WASH LEDERHOSEN

These leather shorts from Austria and Germany are much worn by Aspen children.

The secret to washing them is to use ABSOLUTELY no heat in either the washing or drying cycles.

Don't wash the suspenders, unbutton and take off.

Use cold water in the washing machine with a small amount of wash soap or Woolite. Wash as a usual cycle, then use a fabric softener in the final cold water rinse.

Set the dryer on ''Air'' (no heat) and run for two cycles.

KNIT TOE SOCK

Using knitting worsted (2 oz.) on #6 double-pointed (round) needles, cast on 72 stitches. Knit two, purl two in ribbing for 10 rows. Divide stitches in half, placing markers on each side for decreasing. After ribbing, begin decreasing one stitch on each side of each marker every round until 8, 10, or 12 stitches remain (depending on size of foot). Pull drawstring through remaining stitches and fasten tightly on wrong side. Crochet or braid ties 14" to 18" long, loop once around cast and tie around ankle. Knit plain or work in your favorite pattern.

CONNIE NOSTDAHL

In her Scandinavian Design Shop, Connie sells yarn, and then gives knitting instruction.

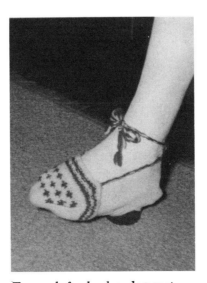

Toe sock for broken leg cast.

JENS AND GLADYCE CHRISTIANSEN

Their ranch up Owl Creek is so beautiful — many TV and magazine advertisements are photographed there.

GLADYCE'S PICKLED PEACHES

12 pounds peaches
3 cinnamon sticks
2 tablespoons whole cloves
4 pounds sugar
1 pint vinegar

Put sugar, vinegar and cinnamon sticks into large kettle. Bring to boil slowly (so as not to scorch) and boil 10 minutes.

Peel peaches and stick three cloves into each peach.

Drop fruit into liquid and cook slowly until tender. Pack in hot, sterilized jars and keep hot. Boil liquid down until quite heavy and pour into jars over peaches. Seal.

JENS' DANDELION WINE

Put 4½ quarts dandelion blossoms into an earthen crock.

Pour 6 quarts of boiling water over blossoms.

Let stand 36 to 48 hours and strain off liquid. Discard the blossoms.

Add to liquid:

1 cake Fleischmann's yeast dissolved in 1 cup warm water.
2 oranges thinly sliced
3 lemons thinly sliced

4½ lbs. sugar. Mix all together. Let stand in crock until it quits fermenting and fruit goes to bottom. Siphon off liquid into wooden keg or glass containers. Cork tightly.

SEWING HINTS

To prevent tangled thread in hand sewing, always knot the end of the strand that leaves the spool first. When using double thread, measure and cut each strand so they go in the same direction; do not simply double in the middle as they will then work against each other.

To "antique" white lace, soak in tea.

Use dental floss to sew on buttons that have a tendency to cut regular thread. This is especially good with metal buttons that often have sharp edges.

Use cornmeal to clean fur pieces.

When sewing a hem by hand, take extra stitches as though ending the hem every few inches. If the hem comes loose, these stop points make it unnecessary to resew the entire hem.

To gather a long length of ruffle, stitch in sections and draw up each section separately. Prevents thread breakage.

JANE CLICK

She sells handmade and custom designed clothing and many other handmade items in her shop Geraniums 'n Sunshine, located in the Mill Street Station.

WILDFLOWERS FOREVER

Whenever on a horseback ride or hike, Peggy carries a book along to press flowers in.

"I learned it from my Grandfather Frederick Cooper who took hikes, always carrying a book for pressing flowers. He then made scrapbooks with collections of the wild flowers from the Aspen area . . . and mixed in family photographs." Peggy treasures the scrapbooks today.

With her pressed flowers, she imbeds them in clear plastic for place mats and makes picture arrangements (buying the frames in Hesteds).

PEGGY ROWLAND

You'll meet her on horseback away up on mountain trails. She likes to ride on pack trips up Hunter Creek Valley, past Reudi, or over East Maroon Pass.

DOUGH FOR CHRISTMAS DECORATIONS OR WHATEVER

4 cups flour
1 cup salt
between 1¾ and two cups water.

Mix altogether and knead for 20 minutes. Shape into decorations. Or use cookie cutters to make your designs. Put on greased cookie pan, bake at 350 degrees for 1½ hours. Paint and varnish.

BEVERLY MOORE

Our artist neighbor, Bev is a partner in Ashley-Moore, an advertising agency, and publisher of *Aspen Magazine* and *Snowmass Affairs*. She and her children, Tracey and Brad live kitty-corner from us.

PLASTER SCULPTURE

Soak plaster board in water until paper covering is soft (about one hour). Peel off paper on one side. While plaster is still damp, carve design with chisels or knives.

JEFF KENTZ

A great hiker on Aspen High School Outdoor
Education trips to the Canyon lands in Utah. Jeff
often made the Granola for the group.

JEFF'S GRANOLA

In a medium speed blender mix
- ⅔ cup water
- 1½ cup corn oil
- 1½ cup honey
- 3 tablespoons vanilla
- 1 tablespoon salt

Mix separately in a giant bowl
- ⅔ pounds rolled oats
- 2 cups wheat germ
- 2 cups shredded coconut
- 2 cups chopped cashew nuts
- 2 cups sunflower seeds
- ½ cup millet
- ½ cup sesame seeds
- 1 cup puffed millet

Slowly add liquid, mix until all is
moistened. Spread on cookie sheet ¾-
inch thick. Bake at 250 degrees until
golden. About 1 to 1½ hours. Add a lot
of raisins after cooking and brown sugar
to your sweet taste. Will keep you going
for hours on a hike.

BRIGITTE ULRYCH

She and her husband, Andre Ulrych, own Andre's Restaurant which is noted for its windowful of blooming flowers (no matter how snowy the weather) and the hanging baskets of green plants.

GREEN ROOMS

Brigitte's recipe for growing plants is: light, water, and attention.

"Although the conditions are adverse for the plants in the restaurant . . . the loud music, no consistent heat . . . they all do well. I think this is because I talk to them. I spend a lot of time with them. It is like meditation for me," she says.

Brigitte also likes to have cut flowers in the house on winter days. "It may seem extravagant to have fresh flowers. But to have them, I'd rather give up something else. For instance, one tea rose will cost no more than a drink.

"Love the cut flowers as much as the potted plants, pay attention to them," she says. "Don't just dump them in a container. Especially with wild flowers, change the water every day and they will last longer." She says if you break at the joint, they will keep better.

"If you are picking wildflowers, carry a knife so you don't jar the roots. Pay attention that you don't pick all in one clump, pick only a few, so the flowers can come to seed and continue in the area."

RAMONA MARKALUNAS

A bright interest in Aspen history and its
people has made Ramona President of the
Aspen Historical Society for many years.
She gives her recipe on how to run the
Society and the Stallard House Museum.

MUSEUM ALA HISTORICAL

Ingredients:
1 well-loved Victorian home on Bleeker Street in Aspen, Colorado
Time and advice of hundreds of congenial volunteers
Many generous contributions of well seasoned furnishings,
    "things," photographs, and money
Scores of visitors
1 fastidious caretaker

With the assistance of hundreds of congenial volunteers of
time and advice, to 1 well-loved Victorian home, gradually add
well-seasoned furnishings and "things."

Season with numerous photographs and documentation in
exhibit form.

Combine, blend and hold together with a generous sprinkling
of money, patience, interest and humor.

Place finished product in a spacious garden area and display
for scores of visitors to assimilate.

Preserve and care for daily by 1 fastidious caretaker. Makes
many delicious servings for today, tomorrow and many years in the
future. With a little special care and continual additions of the same
ingredients, may be enjoyed for generations to come.

ART PFISTER

Art Pfister is an Aspen rancher and great skier. He's also an expert at dowsing...using a forked stick to find underground water. He concentrates and talks to his dowsing device. It responds and turns down...telling Art there is an underground stream of water.

WATER WITCHING

Art explains dowsing, or "water witching."

"It's an ancient practice asking a device a question," he says. "It's an exercise you go through and no one really knows how it works.

"Some people can do it. Some people can't. Usually one out of ten people can do it.

"They can find water, minerals, people, oil."

Art uses a forked stick or plastic in a fork configuration. He explains how it's done:

"You talk to the stick and ask a question. It answers yes or no. If the answer is yes, the stick pulls down. If the answer is no, the stick sits still.

"It's really the concentration that does it."

Art used a forked piece of plastic to show us how it is done.

He talked to the device. He told it he was looking for an underground water line.

He concentrated and kept telling the plastic fork what he was looking for.

And he found our water line.

It's the power of the mind.

Art can learn the depth and amount of water by again asking the forked device yes or no questions, like...how far from the surface is the water...100 feet? 300 feet? Does it flow 365 days a year?

Art says you keep concentrating and asking. The forked device will keep answering by pulling down or staying still. Dowsing is — the proper question is the answer.

CHERIE HISER

Cherie founded and operated The Center of the Eye Photography workshop in Aspen during the 1960s. The center is still spoken of with reverence. Many famous photographers learned their skills there. Cherie shares one of her secrets. Here she is framed in a window at the Hotel Jerome where The Center of the Eye classes were held.

"How to Cut the Photographic Frame" or "The Rule of Thirds"

When framing a photograph in the viewfinder, think of cutting the viewing space into thirds:

then
again

So you have a grid that looks like this in your mind:

Keep all the horizons, action, etc., on those lines. Avoid cutting the frame in half.

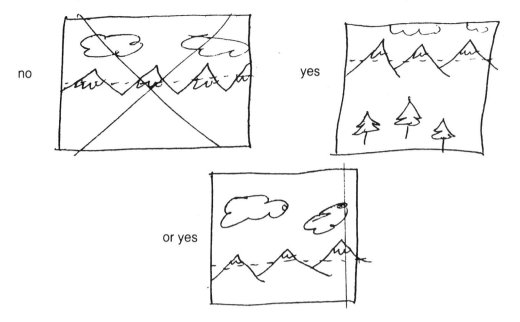

When photographing people...put their eyes on the "third" lines.

It's good to place people/action where the lines intersect:

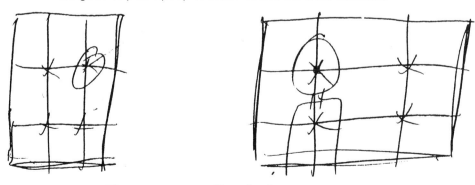

These are compositionally strong areas.

When you learn the "Rule of thirds," then remember to break the rule once in a while, just to "stir up" your photography.

LINDA McCAUSLAND
Linda McCausland is the founder of the Aspen Wildflower Beautification Committee. Under her leadership Aspenites gather wildflower seeds every summer and the seeds are planted along roadsides and on hillsides at the entrances to Aspen. Linda learned all about wildflowers from Aspen landscaper Henry Pedersen and the staff at the Aspen Center for Environmental Studies (ACES) at Hallam Lake.

GATHERING AND PLANTING WILDFLOWER SEEDS

To identify the various kinds of wildflowers, get one of the Rocky Mountain Wildflower books at local bookstores or the Aspen Center for Environmental Studies at Hallam Lake.

Some of the wildflowers that grow in the Aspen area are blue penstemon, blue flax, poppy, blue lupine, white and yellow daisy. This recipe is also the way to collect and plant your hollyhock seeds. The hollyhock and the blue lupine can be picked several times as the flower matures up the tall stalk.

Most wildflowers in Aspen are ready in late August or early September to harvest.

Always leave two thirds of the seeds on a plant...so it can reseed itself.

The seed is ready to harvest when the flower turns brown. Shake the plant a bit and if the seed starts to fall...it's ready. You don't have to separate seeds from flowers because as everything dries, it naturally falls apart.

Put the seeds and dried flowers in a paper bag. Never use plastic because the seeds will rot.

Keep the seeds out in the sun in the bag during the daytime. Carry them inside in evening so dew won't get them wet. The drying is the most important part.

If you have a greenhouse, the seeds can be kept in the greenhouse and you don't have to carry them in and out of the house. Or put them in a sunny window...that works too.

Wildflower seeds do best if planted just before the frost in the fall...October in Aspen. They shouldn't be planted in late summer because there is still too much rain and the seeds will just lay in the ground and rot.

Some people sprinkle their wildflower seeds on the snow just before the springtime thaw. At that time cover with a little compost or straw to help germinate.

Most seeds need the frost to germinate. Frost can be simulated by leaving seeds in the refrigerator for 14 days.

Rake the seeds in lightly to provide good soil contact and prevent the birds from eating them.

Some of the very fine seeds should just be sprinkled on the ground and can be mixed with cornflour or sand to help spread evenly. (These are the ones that also do well sprinkled on the snow.)

Light watering is essential during the hot days in Aspen summer for the first growth season.

Seeds do best in the same type of conditions as the parent plant: i.e., rocky, sandy, shady, moist, etc.

Henry Pedersen is the dean of Aspen wildflowers. Here he is in a bed of his wild daisies.

HINTS FOR ENVIRONMENT
Creating a Healthy World

The environment sometimes seems large and distant, but it really includes our immediate surroundings at home and work, as well as the whole earth system. Everyone makes decisions everyday which add to environmental problems and contribute to their solutions. The vehicles we ride in, the foods we eat, the water we drink and wash with, our clothing, heating, cooling, and the many products we buy and use . . . all of our daily activities impact the planet, both locally and globally.

Here are tips on things each person can do in the daily routine which will help contribute to the solution of our environmental problems. Every person does count.

- In place of toxic furniture polish, use one part lemon juice and two parts olive or vegetable oil on your furniture. To clean glass and windows, use one tablespoon of vinegar in a quart of water.

- Use cedar wood balls instead of moth balls

- Rather than accepting paper or plastic bags at checkout in the grocery, bring your own cotton canvas shopping bags. They are reusable, washable, and made from a renewable resource.

- Plant or sprinkle peppermint, spearmint or pennyroyal around the inside and outside of your home to repel ants. Use cloves or citrus oil (by scratching the surface of an orange or lemon) to repel flies. Grow basil plants around windows and doors to discourage mosquitoes and flies. Place beer-soaked rag, or ½ baking soda and ½ powdered sugar, in a shallow dish overnight to trap cockroaches or silverfish.

- Avoid synthetic building materials in favor of natural products like whole woods, rock, earth and adobe.

- Rethink and try to minimize your auto use. Carpool and use mass transit whenever possible. Rediscover the bicycle and walking . . . great alternatives for commuting, visiting, exercising.

- Weatherize your home and plant trees for shade.

- Use a clothes line rather than a clothes dryer when practical. Run dishwashers only when full and use the energy-saving setting without heated drying.

- Use biomass in the form of plants to clean indoor air. Philodendron, spider plants and aloe vera plants have been found especially effective at absorbing and metabolizing pollutants.

JOHN DENVER

Singer, songwriter, film and TV star, and photographer . . . John Denver is also the founder of The Windstar Foundation, an environmental Think Tank located alongside Snowmass Creek Valley just outside Aspen.

- Don't use disposable diapers. Americans use enough disposable diapers to fill a huge garbage barge every six hours.
- Share magazine and newspaper subscriptions with friends, family and co-workers. When you are finished, donate them to a library, senior center, or other organization.

These hints are among hundreds researched and compiled into booklets called *Creating a Healthy World*. The booklets, written by Beth Richman and Susan Hassol are available through The Windstar Foundation, 2317 Snowmass Creek Road, Snowmass, Colorado 81654.

ASPEN SKI CO. 50TH ANNIVERSARY

In 1997 the Aspen Skiing company held its 50th Anniversary with all kinds of parties on the mountain, in the Sundeck, and at the Hotel Jerome. Aspenites and former Aspenites had such a good time seeing each other again, often for the first time in years.

At one of the cermonies at Lift 1 are members of the Paepcke family, left to right: Nicholas du Brul, Toni Paepcke de Brul, and Maya du Brul.

Ruthie and DRC Brown at the Sundeck.

Olympic skier Stein Eriksen, left, and ski writer Mort Lund confer at one of the Lift 1 parties.

At a luncheon at the Pine Creek Cookhouse are, left to right: Saville Ryan (her father was Ted Ryan who tried to start skiing in Aspen before World War II, Jim Hayes, and Karinjo DeVore.

SKI BUM RELATIONSHIPS

How to maintain a relationship with a hard-core ski bum (in other words, he's a great skier and you're trying your darndest to ski with him more often, but may never ski at his level)

1 cup	Charm
3 cups	Patience
2½ cups	Sugar
1 pinch	Honesty
1 pound	Friendship
5 cups	Sensitivity
1½ cups	Understanding
34	Cuddles
27	Kisses
36	Hugs
112	Lovings
14	Ski Lessons
1 cup	Praise

Mix the Charm, Patience and Honesty into a bowl and stir well. Fold in the Sugar. Blend in Sensitivity and Understanding. Lightly coat pan with Friendship and pour in the mixture. Heat till soft and warm. Serve with Cuddles, Kisses, Hugs and Loving. Throughout the mixture, sprinkle ski lessons from an instructor other than your boy friend. For extra flavor, saturate next date with praise...and a lotta lovin'.

Dedicated to the man who knows.

GINNI GALICINAO

Ginni Galicinao is a retired professional dancer, a fundraiser, and a photographers representative. She serves on the board of the Aspen/Santa Fe Ballet.

LINNEA RILEY

Linnea Riley is one of those people who is so clever with her scissors that she creates magic all around her. Her special talent is called scherenschnitte (paper cuttings with small scissors). She has created a calendar with her paper cutouts called the "Linnea Poster Calendar." Sometimes she works in the *Aspen Times* paste-up department and when things get too hectic, she calms down by cutting out paper dolls.

SWEETHEART CANDY CONTAINERS

To make the Danish Sweetheart candy container for your Christmas tree, cut 2 shapes of equal size from 2 different colors of wrapping paper. Fold in half and cut a slit in each one exactly the same length as the folded edge. Weave the 2 pieces together as shown. Punch hole through the top center, thread with ribbon and fill with candy and hang from the tree.

Danish Sweetheart

The Pasque flower

KAREN MITCHELL

Karen Mitchell designs and creates fabulous gold jewelry.

POLENTA WITH WILD MUSHROOMS

An Italian friend taught Karen this dish when she was living in Milan. It is wonderful in the fall, using fresh local boletus and chanterelle mushrooms. For those of you not experienced in mushroom hunting, dried, wild mushrooms are available in the grocery store. Karen recommends a combination of dried boletus, chanterelle, morel or shitakes.

Polenta

- 3 cups yellow corn meal
- salt and pepper
- 5 tablespoons olive oil
- 1 pound mixed fresh wild mushrooms or/ 4 oz. mixed dried wild mushrooms, soaked in warm madiera and water
- ¼ pound thinly sliced fontina
- ¼ pound thinly sliced gruyere
- freshly grated parmesan

Bechamel Sauce

- 3 cups milk
- 3 tablspoons chopped onion
- ¼ teaspoon white pepper
- ½ teaspoon salt
- 3 tablespoons butter
- 3 tablespoons flour
- pinch grated nutmeg

Preheat oven to 400 degrees. In a large saucepan pour 1½ quarts water and heat. Stir in 1 teaspoon salt and the cornmeal. Bring to a boil under medium heat. Turn boiling mixture to low and cook, stirring for about 5 minutes. Be careful of extremely hot, bubbling polenta. Spoon the mixture into a 8x11.5x2 inch oiled baking dish. Cover dish with foil and bake for about 1 hour. Remove from oven and cool for at least 1 hour.

While polenta is cooling make Bechamel sauce. Melt butter in a small, heavy saucepan. Add onions and cook over medium heat until onions turn golden. Stir in flour. Stir in milk, slowly, and cook, stirring constantly until smooth. Add salt, pepper and nutmeg. Cook over low heat for 20 minutes, stirring occasionally. Strain. Makes about 2½ cups. Bechamel can be made a week or so in advance and kept refrigerated until ready to use.

Saute fresh or soaked dried mushrooms in 3 tablespoons olive oil for about 10 minutes. Reserve a few sauteed mushrooms for topping. Add the rest to the Bechamel sauce.

Slice the cool, pre-baked polenta into long, thin (about ½") strips.

In a lightly oiled oven-proof baking dish, spread some of the Bechamel/mushroom sauce. Cover with strips of cold polenta. Cover polenta with thin slices of gruyere and fontina. Sprinkle with parmesan, salt and pepper to taste.

Continue with layers of sauce, polenta and cheese. Top with remaining sauce and decorate with reserved sauteed mushrooms.

In a pre-heated 400 degree oven, bake mushroom polenta 30-40 minutes. Remove from oven and let cool a few minutes before serving.

MUSHROOM STEW

Fresh store bought mushrooms are good in this but the best are the wild pfifferling, or the grand old man of wild mushrooms, the steinpilz.

Saute ½ a medium onion, finely chopped, in ½ cube of butter. When the onions begin turning color, add 1 pound cut up fresh mushrooms, salt and pepper — continue sauteing another 5 minutes. Add 1 teaspoon dill weed and 1 tablespoon parsley flakes, ½ cup milk, simmer the whole for 10 minutes. At this point the delicious odors become so overpowering, everyone must sit on his hands to resist sampling.

Add ¾ cup sour milk and simmer another 5 minutes. Thicken with flour if you think necessary. Serve over Semmelknodel.

SEMMELKNODEL (Bread dumplings)

In 3 tablespoons butter saute to a golden brown ½ of a finely chopped onion. In a bowl tear 1½ loaves of bread (stale or fresh) into pieces and add to it 1 heaping teaspoon parsley flakes, a dash of Italian seasoning, salt and pepper.

Then mix in 2 beaten eggs and add sauted onion. Dredge the lot with 3 tablespoons flour and moisten it with about 2 tablespoons milk. Knead with hands 'til the dough is well mixed.

Form into balls about 2 inches in diameter (they won't raise), making 4 or 5 dumplings, and then let them stand at room temperature for at least an hour. Any time over doesn't affect them one way or the other. Twenty minutes before the mushroom stew will be done, pop the Semmelknodel into salted boiling water and let bubble away for 20 minutes.

LOUISE GERDTS

In the cubbyhole where she writes. Louise has a summer venture called "The Goldminer's Daughter" — she picks wild mushrooms around Telluride, dries them and sells them to chefs across the nation.

AROUND ASPEN

The Around Aspen column is one of the most popular features in the *Weekly Aspen Times*.

Every chance he gets, Klaus Obermeyer loves to sing and yodel. Left to right are Hans Rieger on the zither, Klaus, and an accordian player.

Dexter Cirillo has written several books about the American Indian arts of the Southwest and often writes about Senator Ben Nighthorse Campbell who is a prominent Colorado silversmith as well as politician.

Aspen Clowns on the Fourth of July.

When Jean Knight left Aspen for Grand Junction, after being a ski bum here for many years, her friends held a farewell luncheon at the Wienerstube. Left to right in the back row are Edie Chisholm, Trudi Ostermier, Jony Larrowe, Mary Dean, Sally Vroom, Connie McCrudden: Middle row: Muriel Frie, Margaret Albouy, Jean Knight, Trudi Baar. In front are Dr. Sherling Lauricilla, Gretl Uhl and Mary Eshbaugh Hayes.

STEFAN ALBOUY

Stefan has kept the silver mining dream alive. He leases and operates the Smuggler Mine (which produced the largest silver nugget in history) and he gives tours of the mine and tells of its history. Stefan grew up listening to the stories of the old miners in Aspen...and he caught their dream.

STEFAN'S MUSHROOM RECIPE

Gather very fresh Boletus (King) mushrooms.

Chop tops and stems into small pieces.

Put butter in a frying pan over the fire, add the tops and stems and then the mushrooms and stir quickly until lightly browned. Salt to taste.

Add as much garlic as you want (lots).

Variation:

Cook as above: add enough half and half cream to make sauce. Season to taste. Make small toasted bread rounds and cover with mushrooms and sauce.

JONY POSCHMAN

In a crazy hat at a midsummer garden party. Jony writes for the *Aspen Illustrated News.*

OREGON GRAPE JELLY

Boil up the berries in enough water to cover and strain juice through a clean cloth.

To 5 cups juice add juice of 1 lemon. Add 1 box of prepared pectin such as Sure-Jell. Bring to hard boil and add 8 cups of sugar. Bring to rolling boil and keep it going for 1½ minutes.

Stir constantly, remove from heat and after removing any scum, pour into sterilized glasses and pour melted paraffin over the top half inch of the jar.

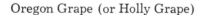

Oregon Grape (or Holly Grape)

ELLIE SPENCE
A favorite family outing each August for the Spence crew —
is to go up in the mountains and gather wild raspberries.

Raspberry

WILD RASPBERRY JAM

Use ¾ cup sugar per cup
of berries. Crush berries, add
sugar, cook down on medium
heat until slightly thickened
(about ½ hour). Put in sterilized jars and seal with paraffin.

CHOKECHERRY JELLY

Watch the chokecherries as they ripen and pick them as black as possible. You can make jelly when they are maroon or dark reddish but the blacker they are, the better the flavor.

Boil berries with enough water to cover. When tender put berries through a seive to separate from pits. Then measure sugar cup for cup — cup of sugar to cup of berry pulp. Cook at rather high heat — a bubbling — stir occasionally. Put a little in a saucer and watch. When it begins to crackle or jell in the saucer, it is done, and can be ladeled into sterilized jars. Cover with paraffin.

MABEL BECKERMAN
For years had The Columbine Lodge — where the Medical Center now stands.

Chokecherry

142

CHOKECHERRY WINE

Pick dark red, ripe chokecherries. Wash.

Measure 1 quart berries and 3 lbs. sugar per each gallon of water.

Boil the water and dissolve the sugar in it. Cool to lukewarm.

Force berries through a colander to separate from pits — then add to water and sugar.

Put in a 50 degree to 60 degree room to begin fermenting. If it doesn't start fermenting in 2 days — add some dissolved yeast. After 6 days begin to taste test each day for sweetness or sourness — when it has the desired taste, then bottle.

After it is bottled, don't seal or cork too tightly for a few days — or it will explode.

DICK STUTSMAN
Earthmoving contractor — with his backhoe.

SERVICEBERRY CONSERVE
(pronounced as Sarvisberry)

4 cups serviceberries
5 cups coarsely chopped, cored, unpeeled, tart apples
6 cups sugar
1 tablespoon grated lemon peel
⅓ cup lemon juice

Wash serviceberries well in cold water — drain. In large saucepan combine with apples, sugar and lemon peel and juice. Cook, stirring constantly, over high heat, until sugar is dissolved. Reduce heat, simmer uncovered, stirring occasionally about 1½ hours, or until mixture is very thick. Remove from heat. Put in sterilized jars right away and seal with paraffin.

LORNA WADDINGTON
Even the oldtimers will tell you — Lorna makes the best serviceberry jelly in town.

Serviceberry

SERVICEBERRY PIE

Lena always puts up a few jars of these berries every Fall — she finds a serviceberry pie is a real treat in the Spring when she hopes Summer may be on it's way.

For canning the berries — To each 2 cups of serviceberries use ½ cup sugar and enough water to cover the berries in the pan. Boil only about 5 minutes — enough to get them tender — but not so long as to lose their delicate flavor. Put up in mason jars.

Then in the Spring — make a piecrust of 1 cup lard, 3 cups flour, salt, a little less than ½ cup water, mix and roll. Use 2 cups of your canned serviceberries and another ½ cup sugar. Some lemon juice for tartness — about ¼ to ½ lemon — don't overdo or will lose the flavor of the wild berry. Then sprinkle over the berries a little flour to thicken. Bake.

Lena's front door.

LENA VAN LOON
She can tell you many stories of Aspen's past.

LAURI LE JUNE HAYES

From a patch of rhubarb that grows in the alley, Lauri makes this punch — rhubarb grows in every alley and vacant lot in town.

RHUBARB PUNCH

Use a quart of rhubarb, cut up — leave skins on to give pink color — and enough water to not quite cover rhubarb. Simmer 'til soft, then add sugar — about ½ cup — to your taste, or honey. Strain and add the juice to ginger ale. Or add it to a lemonade made of juice of 2 lemons, 3 oranges, sugar to taste and a quart of water.

146

AMELIA TRENTAZ

After years of being a ranch wife, Amelia now enjoys being a library assistant.

Rhubarb

RHUBARB-CHERRY PIE

Pastry for 2 crust pie

2 cups pitted sour pie cherries

2 cups cut up rhubarb

1½ cups sugar

6 tablespoons flour

¼ teaspoon nutmeg

Line nine inch pie pan with pastry. Combine cherries, rhubarb, nutmeg, flour and sugar. Mix well. Pour into pastry. Cover with pastry and bake at 400 degrees until done.

SPICED CRABAPPLES (from Mrs. Jurick)

Syrup

4 cups sugar

2 tablespoons stick cinnamon

2 tablespoons whole cloves

1¼ cup apple cider vinegar

¾ cup water

Combine sugar, vinegar, water and spices and boil 10 minutes.

Select firm, well-ripened crabapples. Wash. Do not pare or remove stems. Remove blossom ends. Prick skins to prevent fruit bursting. Cook slowly, until tender in the syrup. Pack in sterilized jars. Fill jars with boiling syrup. Seal.

Crabapple

JOHN AND LUCILLE JURICK

For years they ranched up Snowmass — now have a home in town and Mrs. Jurick has a nursery for children and John gardens.

TO TRANSPLANT ASPEN'S YELLOW ROSES

You transplant the new rose shoots in August — after the mother plant has finished blooming and the sap has gone back down into the roots. Or, if you can mow around them the rest of the summer — you can transplant the year old shoots the next Spring before the bushes leaf out.

GREG KONRAD

An astrologer who looks into the future for many Aspenites, Greg also often peers into the future of Aspen as a city. He says Aspen's destiny is to always be a world-famous resort. Here Greg is with his Ford Galaxy.

RASPBERRY JAM

Greg says this jam is best if made with your homegrown raspberries, but storebought will do.

Purchase 12 jam jars and their two-piece metal tops.

For two batches of jam, use three quarts and one-half pint of raspberries.

Before you start jam, put the 12 jars in dishwasher and run through cycle.

Begin one batch of jam. Make one batch at a time, don't double up recipe. Each batch fills 6 of the jars.

Rinse raspberries gently, place on paper towels.

Put 1½ quarts raspberries into large pan, mash as you go.

Measure three full cups raspberries and put in 5 quart stainless steel pan. Slowly stir 1 oz. or 2 tablespoons and 2 teaspoons of (MCP) Pectin. Let stand for minute and slowly stir in. Make sure all dissolved.

At this point put on another quart pan 2/3 full water to sterilize lids. Throw in 6 lids and sealers.

Turn Jam on high heat, stirring constantly. You can't stop for anything. Bring to a full boil and add 4 cups sugar.

Keep stirring while adding sugar. When comes to full boil again, stir on high heat exactly 4 minutes. Keep stirring constantly. Once 4 minutes is up, stir for another 30 seconds.

Take 6 jars out of dishwasher and the 6 lids that are sterilized.

There are 6 jars left in dishwasher.

Set the 6 jars up, pour jam into jars with a measuring cup.

Fill each jar up, leave ⅛" from top of jar.

Before sealing, wipe off rim of jars. Wax sealing not necessary.

Use tongs and put lids on jars, tighten the lids. Turn over jars for 3 minutes. . . this will seal the lids without wax.

Then turn jars back and let cool.

If the 6th jar is only half full, use it to start next batch. . . or put on vanilla ice cream.

150

SHARON PRIOR

Sharon lives in a lovely Victorian house on Hallam Street. Every autumn she picks crabapples on the grounds of the Aspen Institute for Humanistic Studies and makes this delightful jelly and butter.

CRABAPPLE BUTTER

Cooked pulp of crabapples   Cinnamon
Sugar   Cloves
Lemon Juice   Allspice

After the jelly has been made, put the contents of the jelly bag through a fine sieve. Measure it and allow ½ to ¾ C sugar for each cup. Add spices to taste and the lemon juice. Bring these ingredients to the boil point. Chill. Stir into them a little dry white wine or plain apple cider. Place about ¾ of the puree in a large heatproof crock. Keep the rest in reserve. Put the crock into a cold oven. Set the oven at 300 ° and permit the apple butter to bake until it thickens. As the puree shrinks, fill the crock with reserved apple butter. When the butter is thick, but still moist, put into sterile jars.

CRABAPPLE JELLY

½ grocery bag of crab apples
Sugar
Water
Lemon Juice

Wash apples, remove stems and blossom tips. Cut apples in halves. Add water to barely cover and cook until soft. Crush lightly, put into a jelly bag and let drip overnight. (Important: Don't squeeze bag-it makes the jelly cloudy.) Next day measure juice and boil rapidly for 2 to 3 min. Add ¾ cup of sugar for each cup of juice, and juice of 1 lemon. Stir until sugar is completely dissolved, then boil rapidly for 15 min. Remove from heat, skim, pour into hot, sterilized glasses. Seal.

Harebell

Mountain air dried weeds

WINTER BOUQUETS

The mountain air of Aspen dries some wildflowers and most weeds to perfection — just pick them in August — hang upside down until ready to arrange.

Here is a recipe for preserving the more delicate blossoms such as the wild blue harebell or your garden sweetpeas, with all their color. Cover bottom of shoe box with layer of table salt, place in flowers, laying flat. Spoon salt in, filling in under flowers, to maintain their shape. Cover completely with salt, spooning in gently. Leave at least a week.

For a spray of golden Aspenleaves — use a solution of 2 parts glycerine to 3 parts water. Break off your Aspen branch and soak the stem at least a week in the solution.

EGGS CHICKEN & CHEESE

BARBARA LEWIS
She likes to have prepared meals ahead in the freezer for when husband Bob suddenly brings a group of fellow scientists home to dinner.

GNOCCHI

This Italian dish is a good substitute for potatoes, rice and the usual. It especially goes well with lamb. **And** can be made ahead and kept in the freezer.

2 cups milk	4 tablespoons butter
½ cup yellow corn meal	2 eggs, well beaten
2 teaspoons sugar	1 cup Parmesan or Swiss
1 teaspoon salt	cheese, grated

Scald milk in double boiler. Stir in corn meal gradually. Add salt and sugar. Cover and let stand on low heat for 20 minutes. Remove from heat, add half the cheese, half the butter and the eggs. Spread about ½" thick in greased, shallow earthenware casserole. Cool and chill overnight, if possible. Or freeze it for future reference. When ready to bake spread remaining half cup of cheese and 2 tablespoons butter over top and bake at 375 degrees for 30 minutes.

TRUDY BAAR
She and her husband, Curt, ran a summer children's camp for many years — they are now owners in Tom's Market.

Winter Gingerbread

QUICHE LORRAINE (a cheese pie)

This is a meal in itself and is best served with a green garden salad and wine.

1 ten inch pie shell
6 slices bacon, fried crisp
5 eggs, beaten
2½ cups cream
2 tablespoons melted butter
2½ teaspoons minced onion
1½ teaspoon salt

1¾ teaspoon Worcestershire sauce
¼ teaspoon nutmeg
1 lb Swiss cheese, coarsely grated
3 tablespoons grated Parmesan cheese

Scatter crumbled bacon on bottom of pieshell. Combine eggs, cream, all ingredients and pour over bacon and shell. Sprinkle with Parmesan cheese and put in 375 degree oven. After 15 minutes lower heat to 325 degrees and bake another 30 minutes or until custard is firm.

FLOSSIE ADAMS

Likes to fix a hearty brunch for her boys before a day of skiing — or Jeep trip through the high country.

BRUNCH EGGS

½ lb fresh mushrooms
   (**or** 1-6 oz. can, sliced)
5 tablespoons butter or oleo
10 eggs
½ cup milk

½ teaspoon salt
¼ teaspoon thyme
⅛ teaspoon pepper
1 tablespoon parsley
   (optional)

Wash fresh mushrooms — slice ½ inch thick thru stem. **Or** drain well the canned mushrooms.

Heat 2 tablespoons butter in large pan — saute mushrooms 'til golden. Remove from pan and keep warm.

Combine eggs, milk, salt, thyme and pepper in large bowl — beat (with an egg beater) till just combined — not frothy.

Heat remaining butter in same pan. Add eggs. Cook over low heat. As eggs cook, lift with a spatula and turn gently. DO NOT STIR. Cook till almost set. Stir in mushrooms. Remove from pan and serve. Sprinkle with parsley.

156

MEXICAN EGGS

Ingredients:

8 to 12 eggs

12-oz. size of medium hot salsa

8 oz. tomato sauce

4 oz. aged cheddar sauce

Mix salsa and tomato sauce in a 10 to 12 inch frying pan (deep) and bring to a boil. Break the eggs evenly in the boiling mixture and cover, cooking at a medium heat until the whites are cooked. Shred the cheddar and spread evenly over the top of the mixture for another minute or two so the cheese melts. Serve salsa and eggs with a deep spoon. Serves four to six souls.

WALT SMITH

Walt has been playing jazz piano in Aspen and Glenwood Springs since the 1950s. He has belonged to several groups including The Tipplers and he also plays solo. Here's his recipe for Mexican eggs that he fixes outdoors when camping or for guests in the back yard.

Walt is another of those Aspenites who says the swimming pool at the famous Hot Springs in Glenwood has kept him sane all of these years.

GEORGENE HALL

Georgene is one of those college kids who dropped out to ski bum in Aspen and work in subscriptions and front office at the **Aspen Times**. She went back to college and to a good job in the real world. However, here is a recipe for a dish she always brought to our potluck **Times** parties...it was always a hit.

BROCCOLI ONION AND CHEESE DELIGHT

Serves four.

4 cups broccoli flowers

2 cups chopped red onion

4 tablespoons flour

2 tablespoons butter

½ teaspoon salt

dash pepper

dash garlic

1 cup whole milk

3 oz. cream cheese

1/3 cup grated parmesan cheese

1 cup Italian bread crumbs

Steam broccoli flowers until tender (do not overcook). Saute chopped red onions in butter until tender (do not overcook). Set broccoli and onions aside.

In saucepan melt butter. Blend in flour. Add milk all at once. This should be done on low heat. Stir until thick and bubbly. While stirring, add salt, pepper and garlic powder. Add cream cheese in small pieces.

Continue stirring until cream cheese is smooth.

Combine vegetables and sauce. Bake at 350 degrees for 20 minutes in 1½ quart casserole dish without top. After 20 minutes take out and sprinkle on parmesan. Pat down with wooden spoon. Add Italian bread crumbs. Bake another 20 minutes.

CHEESE FONDUE

Served at Dunaway Chalet in Chamonix during summer of 1953 when Dunaway made first ski descent from summit of Mont Blanc with Lionel Terray for Terray's famous film, "La Grande Descente," winner of 1st prize at Trente Film Festival, Trente, Italy, Fall of 1953.

Brown butter in enamel covered or earthen pot.

Cut up ½ clove garlic and 2 or 3 scallions and brown in butter.

Mix in cut up or chunks of good Swiss cheese, Gruyere or Ementhal and heat with a little white wine to keep from sticking.

Heat slowly — add more white wine to keep in semi-liquid state.

When all heavy liquid, add about ½ cup Kirsch mixed to paste with white flour and a spoonful of arrowroot.

Grate some nutmeg over top.

Serve over low flame to keep bubbling as you and your friends dip French bread. Serve with white wine. Play by ear for your taste and texture.

BIL DUNAWAY
Publisher of
The Aspen Times

OLIVE AMES MOWE
Jazz pianist, fabulous party giver, jetting here and there —
that's Olive.

CHICKEN SUPREME

Have two frying chickens cut up. Flour chicken and brown in electric skillet with mazola oil to about cover half the chicken. When brown, turn skillet to simmer.

With mortar and pestle grind all together (makes about ⅔ cup in all) paprika, black pepper, rosemary, salt, thyme, dill weed, sweet basil, crushed red pepper, taragon and parsley flakes. Sprinkle half over chicken — save other half of spices so when you turn the chicken you can put remainder on. Sprinkle the juice of half a lemon over chicken and add 2 cupfuls of white cooking wine. Simmer about 2 hours — or slow down skillet and cook all evening if the conversation is going great and you want to eat later. Add two tablespoons Sherry wine in the last 45 minutes of cooking.

MARGARET (MIGGS) AND DICK DURRANCE

The Durrances are two of Aspen's most famous photographers. Miggs photographs people and specializes in travel and skiing photos. Dick is a pioneer ski filmmaker.

MEXICAN CHICKEN CASSEROLE

Add celery tops, salt, pepper corns and fresh parsley to a large kettle of water.

Simmer 2 whole chickens in this until just tender.

Cool chickens and remove meat, discarding the skin.

Cut chicken pieces into bite size and place in a large casserole dish.

Break 8 corn tortillas into bite size pieces and mix with chicken.

Add 1 can cream of mushroom soup and 1 can cream of celery soup, 1 can of El Paso tomatoes with green chiles, one cup of chicken stock, and 1 roll of Kraft nippy cheese. Mix all these together. Salt to taste.

Saute ½ lb. of fresh mushrooms and add.

Bake for 45 minutes at 350 degrees.

Add 1 cup grated sharp cheese and 2 small cans of sliced black olives in the last five minutes of baking.

Makes 10 servings.

PETER O'GRADY

Some of the most elegant and delicious meals you will be served in Aspen are by Peter O'Grady Creative Catering. Peter is also one of Aspen's best tap dancers.

CHICKEN BREASTS WITH APPLE AND ROASTED RED PEPPERS

Peter created this recipe on the arm of the Escalante River, Lake Powell, during a week of delightful camping and meandering, with the fabulous golden autumn weather. Serve with a fall salad of tart greens, walnuts, and orange vinaigrette.

The recipe serves two or three, depending on appetite.

2 chicken breasts, 8 oz. each
3 cloves garlic
½ onion, small
1 green apple
15 mushrooms, medium
salt and fresh ground pepper
1 small branch fresh thyme
3 tablespoons Cognac
½ cup fruity white wine
1 red pepper, roasted and peeled
4 slabs Regianno Parmesan
olive oil for sauteing
wheat flour for dredging

Cut red pepper into strips. Set aside. Skin and trim chicken breasts. Set aside in refrigerator. Pluck thyme and chop briefly. Set aside. Cut apple in wedges.

Cut garlic into slabs. Brown in 3 tablespoons olive oil over medium flame. Discard garlic. Slice onion into half rounds. Slice cleaned mushrooms into quarters. Add onion, mushrooms, and apples to olive oil and saute over medium flame for 7 minutes. Add wine, cover pan, and reduce heat and simmer for 10-15 minutes, or until soft. Remove to covered bowl. Recipe can be done in advance to this stage.

Dredge chicken breasts in wheat flour. Heat saute pan with 3 tablespoons olive oil. Add chicken breasts to hot oil. Brown and turn. Remove from pan. Do NOT cook chicken more than halfway.

Wipe pan clean. Add 3 tablespoons butter. Heat over medium flame. When warm, add onion/mushroom/apple mixture. Place chicken breasts on top. Cover and simmer, adding liquid if necessary, until chicken breasts are heated through, about 5 minutes.

To finish, place slabs of Parmesan on chicken and place under broiler to glaze the cheese, or cover again and steam to melt. Uncover, add Cognac and ignite, to the delight of the waiting diners.

And to think Peter prepared this on a camping trip!

GREEK CHICKEN

Chicken breasts — wash and dry thoroughly. In paper bag mix flour, salt and pepper. Shake chicken pieces individually in bag to coat with flour mixture. Shake off any excess flour.

In casserole (or frying pan, or electric frying pan can brown and bake nicely) melt butter and brown chicken pieces (skin side first). Season with salt, pepper, onion or garlic salt. Place lemon slices in bottom of casserole, bay leaf also. Pour Vermouth or dry white wine (about ¼ cup) over chicken.

Cover and bake for about an hour at 350 degrees. Uncover and baste 'til juices cook down. (If not brown enough, broil for few minutes). Serve with rice.

Inside the Durant mine.

MOLLY HENEGHAN

An Aspen teacher — now an Architect's wife.

KIM HOWELL HARDY
With daughter Eva.

CHICKEN POT PIE

2 packages of frozen, cooked, cubed chicken — or at least 3 cups of chicken cooked and cut in pieces.

SAUCE

1 can mushroom soup   ½ lb sharp cheese, grated
⅓ cup white wine (Sauterne)   1 teaspoon Worcestershire sauce

Blend all together with blender or egg beater.
Pour sauce over chicken in shallow pan.
Preheat oven to 425 degrees.
Place refrigerator biscuits on top of the chicken and sauce and bake at 425 degrees for about 12 minutes — until sauce is bubbly and biscuits golden brown. Serve chicken and sauce on top of biscuits.
Serve with salad or vegetable.

D BAR TEN CHICKEN

If you wish to be prepared for an outdoor picnic in advance and be ready to be able to cook the chickens in about five (5) minutes, we suggest you do the following:

Cut chicken in half
(removing the back is optional)
Cook in the oven for 35 minutes at 425°
OR
Boil in chicken stock for 10 to 15 minutes

REMOVE and place the chicken in the following marinade for 24 to 48 hours.

Marinade:
    ½ cup of olive oil
    Juice from one (1) lemon
    1 clove of garlic (crushed)
    2 Bay leaves
    1 bunch of Bay leaves
    1 bunch of fresh Rosemary
    Salt and pepper to taste

Roast or broil till hot or cooked thoroughly.

CHUCK DUNBAR
Chuck Dunbar is a broker for newspapers and other media. Here he is with His daughter, Debbie.

165

DICK TUCK
Dick Tuck is famous as a political puckster. Over the years as a writer in Washington, DC and in Aspen. . . he has especially enjoyed playing pranks on President Richard Nixon.

DICK TUCK'S HOLIDAY HORS D'OEUVRE

As the Nation's guest, I have increased my holiday dinner invitations considerably since I discovered an ideal substitute for the obligatory gift bottle of wine or fruit cake.

When you show up at the festive house with a perfectly cooked goose, you'll find you'll make everyone happy except perhaps the hostess, whose dinner might be upstaged.

For those who are dieting, and who isn't, and to whom the sight of a groaning board is a depressing exercise in self control, the chance to nibble on some slenderizing goose before sitting down to dinner is welcome.

Low-cal goose? Surprised? The secret of cooking delicious goose is the removal of the fat. I've found a foolproof way:

Remove the wings from an 8-10 pound goose and pierce the breast with 5 or 6 pinpoints.

Place on a rack inside a large roasting bag, breast side DOWN.

Add two cups of water. If you can find fresh juniper berries, crush and add them to the water. Better yet, add one quarter cup of good gin. (I suggest you test the quality of gin extensively before deeming it worthy to join the ingredients - or guests - in the bag.)

Seal the bag. Pierce it with a couple of small holes and cook in a 450 degree oven for one hour.

You don't have to stuff the goose, but if you want to throw some apples and/or dried apricots inside the cavity, or spread a little apricot jam on the outside of the bird, go ahead.

ALTERNATE RECIPE: Buy a fully cooked goose and drink the gin.

FREDDIE PEIRCE
With husband Everett, she runs Buttermilk restaurant in winter and
Snowmass Guest Ranch in summer.

CHICKEN IN ORANGE SAUCE

Two 2½ lb fryers, cut up

1½ teaspoons salt

1½ teaspoons paprika

¼ cup margarine

⅓ cup unsifted flour

¼ cup sugar

¼ teaspoon dry mustard

½ teaspoon ground cinnamon

¼ teaspoon ground ginger

2½ cups orange juice

1 orange, pared and peeled

About 1 hour before serving sprinkle chicken with salt and paprika. Brown
a few pieces at a time in margarine in large fry pan. Into drippings stir flour,
sugar, mustard, cinnamon, and ginger 'til smooth. Slowly add orange juice.
Add chicken, simmer, covered, for ½ hour.

Cut off all membrane from orange. Sliver peel, cover with water, simmer
10 minutes, drain. Section orange. Sprinkle orange peel over chicken, add
orange sections, cover. Cook 10 minutes or until fork tender. Serve chicken
with sauce over it.

JOAN LANE
Writes for *The Grand Junction Sentinel*.

CHICKEN BARBECUE

Perfect for picnics in the woods at Joan and Shady Lanes.

Melt some sticks of butter in a pan on the grill where you are barbecue-ing the chicken and stir in garlic salt and parsley. Brush on the chicken as it is cooking.

ELIZABETHCLARE'S CHICKEN VESUVIUS

Chicken parts

    2 pkg thighs with skin

    1 pkg breasts without skin

    2 pkg Italian sausage

olive oil

4-5 cloves garlic

1+ cups fresh parsley

garlic powder

lemon pepper

salt

flour

3+ cups red wine

Coat chicken parts with flour seasoned with salt, pepper and garlic powder. Brown in olive oil and garlic cloves. Set aside in large pot.

Cut sausage links into 1" cubes and brown. Add to chicken. Add diced parsley and wine.

Bake at 350 degrees for 2½ hours. (Use more liquid (wine) at altitude).

Serve with wild rice and a salad. Freezes well.

ELIZABETHCLARE HUNT

ElizabethClare Hunt came framed to a summer Exotic Hat party. Aspen's yellow roses are beautiful in summer or winter.

CHICKEN SANTA FE

Adapted from a 19th Century Northern New Mexico Kitchen

    6 boneless chicken breasts
   juice of one large lime
    2 cloves garlic, crushed
   ¼ tsp cilantro, minced
   salt and pepper to taste
   ½ cup sun-dried tomatoes, softened
       in boiling water for 2-3 minutes
    3 whole chiles —mild, medium, or
       hot; fresh, frozen or canned
   ½ cup goat cheese
   ½ cup tequila

Arrange chicken breasts in baking dish. Squeeze lime juice on top. Mix garlic, cilantro, spread over chicken; add salt and pepper to taste. Dice softened sun-dried tomatoes, sprinkle on top of chicken. Arrange chiles on top of tomato pieces. Crumble goat cheese on top. Pour tequila over casserole. Bake in 350 degree oven for 45-60 minutes, or until done. Serves 6.

Accompaniment: boiled new potatoes with capers, butter, and parsley. Green beans with chopped red onions, red peppers, and toasted sesame seeds.

NANCY WOOD

Nancy Wood lives in Santa Fe but says Aspen is her spiritual home. Every summer she comes and dances at the top of Independence Pass. She is a noted poet, novelist and photographer. Several of her books of poetry, such as "Many Winters" and "Spirit Walker" are combined with the mystical paintings of American Indians done by Frank Howell. Other books of poetry by Nancy are "Hollering Sun" and "War Cry on a Prayer Feather." Photography books include "Taos Pueblo," "The Grass Roots People" and with Roy Stryker "In This Proud Land." Fiction includes "The Man Who Gave Thunder to the Earth" and an anthology of works by American Indians is "The Serpent's Tongue."

BERNIE MYSIOR

Bernie and Donna Mysior. Bernie often plays guitar with local bands, Donna is a tap dancer and a ballet dancer.

CHICKEN A LA MYSIOR

Ingredients

4 chicken breasts or substitute tofu
    for veggie dish

1 can (10 ¾ oz) cream of
    mushroom soup

2 cups rice (uncooked)
    (use broth with water for rice)

1 can chicken broth (14½ oz size)

10 oz Velveeta Cheese — approximately 12 slices, if not the chunk size

4 to 8 oz Colby Cheese (Jack Cheese)

1 tsp seasoned pepper

1 to 2 tablespoons cinnamon

salt to taste

vegetables — either frozen 16 oz or fresh vegetables — any mix desirable

2-3 cloves garlic

olive oil/or butter to taste for browning chicken

Grape Nuts — to top off dish

Method

1. Start rice, using broth
2. Cut chicken into small pieces-approximately ½".
3. Start oil or butter in large sauce pan.
4. Dice garlic and add to oil to brown.
5. Put in chicken and simmer at low to medium heat. Add pepper and cinnamon while simmering
6. If using fresh veggies-start chopping them up. If using frozen veggies, microwave till thawed
7. Cook chicken till done in saucepan-add mushroom soup, next add veggies, then mix in rice. Season to taste (cinnamon is the key).
8. Spray casserole dish with no stick veggie spray.
9. Add Colby Cheese, grated, in saucepan, and mix.
10. Put all in casserole dish.
11. Cover top of dish with Velveeta Cheese evenly and cover dish with heavy duty foil. Bake at 350 degrees for approximately 30 minutes.
12. Take out of oven — take off tinfoil.
13. Cover evenly top of dish with Grape Nuts-may add more Velveeta.
14. Bake until crisp and brown-approximately 10 minutes.

Bon Appetit!

FRANCOIS COUTURIER

Francois Couturier is a fabulous chef. For several years he had The Rocky Mountain Pie Company and this chicken pie was always in great demand.

CHICKEN PIE A LA FRANCOIS

Serves 6-8 people

In a heavy skillet, pour a tablespoon olive oil and cook over moderate heat with 1½ pounds of boneless, skinless chicken thighs, until slightly brown. Set aside to cool.

In the same skillet, on reduced heat, place 1 pound finely chopped shallots with a cup of dry white wine. Let simmer about 20 minutes.

In the meantime wash and slice about 1½ pounds of fresh mushrooms.

When shallots are getting soft and translucent transfer them to a large saucepan.

In the skillet place mushrooms and 1 cup water and let simmer over low heat.

Finely cut the chicken into pieces no bigger than one inch in any dimension and add to the shallots in pan, along with two cups dry white wine. Keep cooking on low heat, then add mushrooms and juices from the skillet when they have reduced enough.

Let simmer another hour, making sure that the mixture is quite moist.

In the end, add another cup dry white wine, 3 tablespoons flour, 8 oz butter, a dash Italian seasoning and salt and pepper to taste.

Take off the stove as soon as mixture thickens. Let cool down completely.

Prepare Your Crust:

In Kitchen Aid Mixer, place 4 oz butter, 3 oz lard, 2 cups white flour, 1 cup whole wheat flour, 1 teaspoon salt and ¼ teaspoon baking powder.

Blend on medium speed with dough hook, until you get pea size chunks.

Add 7 oz water, very cold, and turn the speed up a notch.

In a few seconds dough starts clinging together. Stop blender and gather dough in a ball, then you will place it in a Ziplock bag and chill for at least an hour (overnight is even better).

Roll dough into two 12" rounds. Place one in a 10" pie pan, and fill with cold chicken filling. Place second round on top, fold edges together, making decorative pattern all around pan.

Brush top with 1 beaten egg yolk and decorate top crust with knife, poking a couple of holes.

Bake 45 minutes in oven at 350 degrees F.

Serve hot with a salad mix in vinaigrette sauce.

Bon Appetit!

FRANK TODARO

Frank Todaro is a marvelous piano player (he is in demand at many parties) and he also is an expert about wines.

Since Frank's agile piano-playing fingers didn't show in his portrait...we are showing them here.

FRANK TODARO'S CHICKEN CACCIATORE

1 large chicken cut into pieces
1 diced onion-medium
3 cloves diced garlic
½ bunch celery
1 cup olives, no pits
½ jar capers
1 quart fresh tomato sauce
1 cup red wine

Place onions, garlic, celery and chicken into large pot. Let cook for 15 minutes. Then add tomato sauce, wine, capers and olives. Cover and let cook for 40 minutes. Place chicken and sauce on bed of fresh cooked pasta.

STEVE MUNDINGER

An Aspen photographer, Steve Mundinger shoots all the events for Jazz Aspen/Snowmass as well as many other local events and parties.

CHICKEN ENCHILADAS

(serves six)

Ingredients

24 oz boneless chicken (chopped)

24 oz jar enchilada sauce

1 red bell pepper

1 green bell pepper

2 green anaheim peppers

1 jalapeno pepper

½ onion

24 oz shredded mixed cheddar and
        monterey jack cheese

1-16 oz can refried beans

1 dozen package of flour tortillas

To prepare filling:

Roast the peppers for 20 minutes in the oven at 375 degrees

Saute chicken in a little enchilada sauce until cooked.

Remove peppers from oven and cool in cold water.

Saute chopped onion in enchilada sauce.

Peel skin from peppers and remove seeds.

Chop peppers and add to onions.

Heat refried beans in sauce pan.

Add cooked chicken to peppers and onions.

To assemble:

Start by covering the bottom of a 9x13 cake pan with enchilada sauce (use a second pan if more room is needed). Place tortilla on flat surface and spread 1 oz refried beans in center. Add large spoonful of filling on top of beans. Sprinkle 1 oz shredded cheese on top of filling. Roll up tortilla and place seam down in pan. Repeat until pan is full. Pour remaining sauce on top of enchiladas, sprinkle remaining cheese on top of sauce.

Cooking

Bake at 375 degrees for 30 minutes or until cheese on top is melted and crispy. Remove from oven and let stand for 10 minutes, then serve.

ELLEN GRENKO
Your hostess at Hillside Lodge.

VENISON STEW

Two pounds of cubed venison seasoned with salt and pepper, dredged with flour and browned in bacon fat.

Put in heavy stew pot. Cover with beef boullion and add an equal amount of any dry red wine. Simmer for an hour or more. When meat is almost tender add — for each person — two stewing onions, two carrots. Continue to simmer for a half hour, then add a potato cut into cubes. When potato is done, stew is ready to serve.

Serve with crusty fresh French bread, a green salad and a bottle of good wine.

BARBECUED VENISON ON BUNS

One thing we liked to fix on cook-outs when we had a big bunch was barbecued venison on buns. I cooked venison roast ahead of time, then cut it into small bits. After we got a fire going I put catsup, sliced onion and a **small** amount of vinegar in a big black kettle and heated the meat in it. We ladeled it out on buns and it was a treat.

RUTH RINGLE
She and her husband, Verlin, are former owners of *The Aspen Times.*

JUDY GERBAZ
With daughter, Gina. Everyone told me, "Judy fixes elk the best."

ELK OR VENISON IN THE GERBAZ MANNER

Cube meat in inch size pieces — the amount depending on the number to be served.

Roll meat in flour that has been seasoned with salt and pepper.

Brown well on all sides. Add sufficient water to cover. Bring to a boil. Sprinkle with one packet of French onion soup mix. Simmer 1½ to 2 hours — or all day if you have time. The longer it cooks the better the flavor and the more tender the meat. Thicken with flour before serving. (If you cook it all day, keep adding water and then let it thicken itself into a gravy.) Great served with mashed potatoes, rice or buttered noodles.

FRED AND FLORENCE GLIDDEN

Fred is author "Luke Short," writer of western novels. Florence is a charter member and worker at the Hospital Thrift Shop.

BAKED PHEASANT

Quarter and brown pheasant with chopped onion, as you would chicken. Then cover with sour cream and bake in covered pan or casserole until tender.

The Glidden's Victorian home.

KATY SMITH

Katy's home is in this hayfield up Little Woody Creek Canyon.

ELK JERKY

3-4 pounds meat	2 teaspoons salt	1 cup dry red wine
½ onion, diced	2 cloves garlic	¼ cup worcestershire sauce
¼ teaspoon thyme	2 teaspoons pepper	¼ cup soy sauce
2 bay leaves	½ cup vinegar	¼ cup bottled smoke

CUTTING: Use a cut of sinewy meat from the flank. Trim off all fat (any left turns rancid). Cut, WITH the grain, strips between 6-12 inches long, ⅛-inch thick, and less than 1-inch wide. The meat is easier to cut when it's slightly frozen.

MARINATING: Combine the other ingredients and pour half of marinade over meat strips. Marinate covered for 24 hours (not in refrigerator). Squeeze the strips to get the juices out, throw away juice and then marinate again (in fresh remaining half of marinade) for 24 hours.

DRYING: **Indoors:** Lay the pieces out on your oven racks with a pan underneath to catch the drippings. Leave the meat in the oven with just the pilot light on for 3 or 4 days. **Outdoors:** Set meat strips on a grill or rack and leave in the sun for about 10 hours. To protect hers from animals and insects, Katy put the rack in a large wheelbarrow and covered it with loose screening. It was convenient to roll the wheelbarrow inside if she had to leave the house. When finished, store the jerky in closed container. Can use beef instead of elk.

MAIN DISHES WITH MEAT

EVA GERBAZ

A weekend treat — the drive down to her ranch to get eggs.

In the Spring dry irrigation ditches make good hiking.

ITALIAN SAUSAGE

Ranch size proportions — in this recipe you are to use 25 pounds of meat, ¾ beef to ¼ pork, ¾ elk to ¼ pork, or ¾ venison to ¼ pork. Grind through meat grinder as for hamburger.

Add 1 cup salt, 2 to 3 tablespoons pepper, 2 tablespoons crushed garlic. Mix well and stuff into hog casings (which can be bought at grocery store). Hang and let cure to the hardness you want, or freeze immediately.

KLABASA (Yugoslavian Pork Sausage)

Keith's family made this every year at their ranch. He always made himself a big batch to take down to college while he was studying engineering.

Use about ⅔ fresh pork to about ⅓ **lean** beef. Grind in coarse meat grinder, or better still, cut up meat into small pieces with knife.

Add salt, pepper and garlic water to individual taste.

Let meat with seasoning stand overnight in very cool room.

Stuff into pork casings and let stand overnight again.

Smoke sausage. If done properly (at about 65 degrees F) the meat will have a pink color.

To serve, boil in water for 45 minutes.

Keith's favorite meal consists of these sausages, pan fried potatoes, lettuce with vinegar and oil. No dessert.

KEITH MAROLT
Now an engineer in California, Keith drove trucks for us when we had our earthmoving business.

CELIA MAROLT
She gave a trio of racing greats to the skiing world with her sons, Bud, Max and Billy Marolt.

SLOVENIAN PASTIES (Yugoslavian)

Celia's grandfather, Joe Skriner, carried these meat pies for his lunch when he worked as a miner in the Smuggler.

Dough

1 cup flour   2 eggs   pinch salt

Knead altogether. Roll as for noodles. Be sure and flour rolling area very well or dough will stick.

Filling

About a pound and a half of any left-over meat, or combinations, pork, beef, hamburger.

Grind the meat. Add 1 small onion chopped very fine, salt, pepper, marjoram, rosemary — just a pinch of each. Mix together. Add 1 egg to hold meat mixture together.

Divide into about 5 or 6 portions, lay on rolled out dough, cut around meat portions in triangular shape, fold up like you would a diaper, pinch together. Submerge the pasties into salted water that is barely boiling (do not boil hard as pasties will boil apart) for 20 minutes. Serve hot or cold. Excellent with endive or dandelion greens, wilted with vinegar and bacon.

WILTED GREEN SALAD: Chop or cut up about 5 or 6 strips of bacon, render until crisp. Add about 3 tablespoons vinegar diluted with same amount of hot water. Remove from heat, let cool just a minute, pour over endive or dandelion greens, serve at once.

Old mine buildings.

TERESE DAVID

She has one of the craziest shops you'll ever see — and her clothes designs are world famous.

BOEUF AUX OLIVES

4 lbs. stewing beef
1 can pitted black olives (family size can)
1 large can tomato sauce
1 small can tomato paste
¼ lb. butter (1 stick)
    Any red Burgundy or Claret wine

Cut the stewing beef into cube sized pieces, shake in bag with flour and salt and pepper. Brown the meat in butter, add the tomato sauce and tomato paste and stir. Cover with wine and simmer gently about 1½ hours. Add olives and simmer another half hour. Can be prepared the day before, refrigerated and reheated. Terese says it can be prepared at 2 a.m. and served the next day. Serve with buttered noodles and tossed green salad.

FERNE SPAULDING
With her practical nature — she helps Terese run the shop.

ELEGANT MEATBALLS

With 1½ pounds of hamburger combine ½ cup finely chopped onion, 1½ cups dry bread, 1 teaspoon salt, ½ teaspoon pepper, touch of sage, garlic salt and basil. Dampen with boullion mixed with catsup.

Shape into meatballs and brown. Pour (No. 303) can tomatoes over meatballs and simmer. At last minute stir in sour cream. Serve over rice.

ELLEN HARLAND
A lady architect.

GYPSY GOULASH

Cut into 1 inch cubes about 3 pounds end-cut pork loin. After dusting meat with flour, brown in small amount of bacon drippings. Add one large chopped onion and brown that too. Add 2 tablespoons good Hungarian paprika, salt and pepper, one bay leaf. Then mix in one large can sauerkraut, rinsed in cold water and drained, and one tablespoon caraway seeds. Add enough beef stock to barely reach the top of mixture in the pot. Simmer for at least two hours. Just before serving, add 1 pint sour cream, heat but do not boil. Serve over broad egg noodles.

BEEF ROLL UPS

Have roundsteak cut thin, so you can roll it. Cut into serving pieces. Spread on each piece mustard, chopped onion, bacon (**not** pre-cooked) cut into small pieces, and salt and pepper. Roll up meat and wrap with string, or hold with a toothpick. Brown on all sides in butter, add couple inches of water in bottom of pan. Steam and simmer for about 3 hours or until tender. With juice make a brown gravy and pour over.

ROSA CROSBY GETTMAN

My summer time neighbor for 15 years. Her father, John Crosby, was anesthetist at the Aspen hospital for 40 years.

KEITH SAWVEL
Sculptor and painter.

HAMBURGER CASSEROLE

1 lb. hamburger

1 buffet size can tomato sauce
   (7¾ oz.)

1 cup egg noodles

   salt to taste

clove of garlic, finely chopped,
   for extra flavor

Pour water into electric skillet until half full. Salt. Bring to boil. Sprinkle in noodles and garlic. When water almost absorbed, open hamburger container, give a generous amount to the cat, put the remainder in the skillet. Spread hamburger with medium size palette knife, cook at 375 degrees until rare, medium, or well done. Pour in can of tomato sauce. Simmer a few minutes. This should be eaten from the skillet with palette knife to avoid excess dishwashing.

PATSY H. APPLETON
Gives a recipe for young couples on a budget.

SUPER DUPER HAMBURGERS

1 lb. hamburger
1 onion, chopped
1 egg
  slice bread
1 small can mushrooms

3 shakes garlic salt
2 shakes Worchestershire sauce
  salt
  pepper
1 package onion soup
  water

Combine all ingredients except soup and water in large bowl. Mix well and shape into 4 to 6 large patties. They will be crumbly. Brown without turning about 3 minutes, or until a light brown, in oil or butter on top of stove. Add soup mix and one to two cups water. Cover and simmer on top of stove about one hour. Meat should be well done and gravy dark. If gravy becomes too thick while cooking, add small amount of water. Stir occasionally while cooking to prevent sticking. Serve with baked potato, green beans and salad. Serves 4 to 6.

In the summer the sheep come through town.

LAMB STEW

2 lbs. boneless lamb, cut into bite size chunks	8 carrots, scraped and quartered
½ cup seasoned flour	24 small white onions, peeled
2 tablespoons fat	6 potatoes, pared and quartered
1 clove garlic	1 cup diced celery
1 medium onion, sliced	1 teaspoon salt
1 bay leaf	½ teaspoon marjoram

Dust meat well with ½ cup seasoned flour placed in paper bag. Heat garlic with fat in 4 quart saucepan or Dutch oven with tight fitting lid. Brown meat a few pieces at a time. Pour off any excess fat — return all browned meat to pan. Add enough boiling water just to cover meat — add sliced onion and bay leaf. Cover tightly. Bring to boiling, reduce heat to simmer, stirring occasionally, 1½ hours. Add carrots, onions, potatoes, celery, salt and marjoram. Simmer 25 minutes or until meat and vegetables are tender. In order to thicken the gravy, 2 tablespoons of flour may be added — cook mixture over low heat, stirring constantly until gravy thickens.

ALBINA GERBAZ
When the children were little, Bena would always give a helping hand.

DANNY BARRY
Aspen's Irishman cowboy.

IRISH TURKEY

A hearty, working man's meal.
Boil a 4 or 5 pound brisket of corned beef in water to cover for 4 hours. When meat becomes tender add potatoes and cabbage and keep boiling until vegetables done. Serve altogether with broth.

Calf roping.

BECKY NOONAN
Ski instructor — used to fly with the airlines as a stewardess.

BOILED DINNER

Boil ham hocks (have them cracked at market) in water to cover for several hours. Add whole cloves, basil, odds and ends of spices. Always a pinch of sugar. Many different vegetables may be used. Of course potatoes and onions are a must. Along with cabbage. Don't overcook the cabbage — it goes into the pot last. Don't forget to have vinegar on the table.

This is delicious made in a big iron pot. I always just put the pot and all on the table. Serve with French bread.

BARBARA SIMMONS
A friendly Aspen salesgirl.

SWEET AND SOUR PORK (or Meatballs)

Sauce

1½ cups liquid (water and pineapple juice)

⅓ cup vinegar

⅓ cup brown sugar

2 tablespoons corn starch

2 tablespoons soy sauce

Cook sauce 'til thick, add pineapple tidbits (the tall thin can), one bell pepper cut in wedges, one small onion cut in wedges.

Cook pork or use leftover pork roast, or use meatballs. Put cooked meat into sauce and heat through. About 5 minutes. Vegetables must be crisp. Serve over rice.

LAMB SUZI

Cut lamb shank in chunks, brown with flour, salt, pepper, minced garlic, rosemary, and chopped onions. Add small can of tomato sauce and red wine and cook for two hours. Serve over noodles.

Tree carvings in Weller Lake campground.

SUZI JACOBIE

Ski instructor in the winter — she works in Aspen shops during the summer.

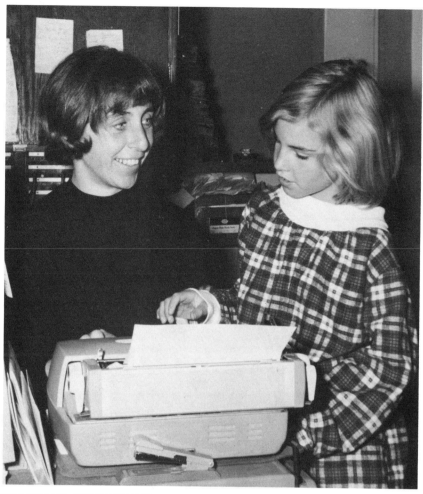

MARIAN MELVILLE
Busy at the Mountain Chalet.

CHALET VEAL

This recipe slowly evolved in our kitchen, partly because our grocer carries the meat as a standard item, and partly because we tried varying Veal Parmesan.

8 veal patties (the cubed steak type, that are usually about 25c each)
8 thin slices cooked ham
8 thin slices Swiss cheese
1-2 tablespoons bacon fat

4 oz. can mushrooms, stems and pieces
3 tablespoons flour
1½ cups water (use the mushroom juice as part)
16 toothpicks

Place one slice of ham and one of Swiss cheese on the veal patty. Roll very carefully so the meat stays intact. (If it does tear, it will cook successfully anyway.) Secure with two toothpicks. Brown in bacon fat. Remove meat rolls. Make gravy by mixing the flour in cold water and mushroom juice. Then add to pan and stir until thickened. Do not add any seasonings. The ham and cheese do all the seasoning. Return meat to pan. Cover with mushrooms and simmer 10 minutes. Serve with rice. Serves 6 to 8. This can be made ahead, put in a casserole, refrigerated, then heated in the oven about an hour at 350 degrees.

GERDA SEVERIN HINN
Gives one of her family recipes from Denmark.

FRICADELLER (DANISH MEAT BALLS)

1 lb. ground round

2 pork chops
   (grind meat together)

2 eggs

1 cup milk

1 medium onion, finely chopped

  salt and pepper

1 tablespoon Worcestershire sauce

Blend all ingredients well — stirring to a smooth consistency. Then add 1 cup fine bread crumbs and 1 tablespoon parsley leaves (chopped) and blend again, adding small amount of milk if necessary to a smooth consistency. Drop by tablespoons into hot oil or fat just covering skillet bottom and cook over medium heat until done, turning only once. They should be brown and crisp on each side. Takes about 45 minutes. Make gravy from drippings, adding flour and milk and chopped parsley, and at the last moment before serving add 2 tablespoons of Sherry.

JAN HABBERLEY

A ski instructor, Jan lived several years in Kitzbühel, Austria, where she got this recipe.

TIROLERLEBER (Tirolian Liver)

3 tablespoons oil

1 lb. calves liver, cut in strips 2″ wide
  flour

½ cup chopped onion

¼ cup stock (or water with bouillon cube)

1 sour pickle

2 to 3 tablespoons capers

2 tablespoons chives

2 tablespoons parsley

1 to 1½ cups sour cream

Lightly dredge liver strips in flour. Brown quickly in oil. Remove liver from pan and saute finely chopped onions until soft. Put meat back into pan with stock or water. When liver is cooked, add pickle, capers, parsley and chives, all finely chopped together. Add sour cream. Mix well, simmer and serve with noodles.

DOLORES STUTSMAN
She uses her homemade sausage on this pizza — see Eva Gerbaz' recipe on page 76.

PIZZA PIE

Dissolve 1 package yeast in 2 cups warm water. Stir in 2 teaspoons sugar, 3 teaspoons salt, 4 tablespoons olive oil. Stir in 6 cups flour. Knead. Place in greased bowl. Cover, let rise 1½ hours.

Punch dough down — divide into 6 equal pieces and roll out for pizza pans, place in ungreased pans.

Sauce: 2 cans tomato paste, 4 small cans tomato sauce, salt, pepper, pinch of marjoram, oregano and thyme, and 2 cloves of minced garlic. Stir well. Divide equally on dough.

Grate 1½ lbs. cheese — half Mozarella, half sharp. Spread over sauce.

Grind up 2½ lbs. polish sausage. Spread over cheese. (Dolores uses her homemade venison sausage.)

Top with canned mushrooms and sliced black olives. Bake at 400 degrees for 20 minutes. Leave on lowest rack half the time — so bottom will be brown.

INA CLAIRE McTARNAGHAN
A nurse who loves to ski.

SKIER'S QUICK VEAL PARMESAN

This recipe takes only about 20 minutes.

4 to 6 veal cutlets (the patty type)
flour
tomato sauce, small can
salt and pepper to taste
leaf oregano
Parmesan cheese, grated
Mozarella or Provolone cheese

Flour, then brown veal cutlets in a little oil, drain oil off. Salt and pepper and sprinkle oregano and Parmesan cheese on top.

Pour tomato sauce over and simmer about 10 to 15 minutes. Before serving place a slice of Mozarella or Provolone cheese on top of each cutlet. Cover and heat 'til cheese melts. Good with French bread, salad and Italian green beans. Serves 4 to 6.

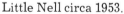

Little Nell circa 1953.

BETTE STROUD
You'll meet her at the Golconda.

TAGLARININ

1 lb. elbow macaroni (cooked)

1 lb. hamburger

2 tablespoons olive oil

2 cloves garlic, chopped

1 dozen ripe olives

   salt and pepper

2 bay leaves

1 tablespoon chopped parsley

1 can mushrooms

½ lb. American cheese, chopped

1 large can tomatoes

1 teaspoon chili powder

   grated Parmesan cheese

1 can corn niblets

Brown meat in olive oil with garlic, parsley and mushrooms. Mix with everything else except Parmesan cheese. Cook on top of stove **slowly** for ½ hour. Stir occasionally. Put in casserole with grated Parmesan cheese on top. Bake uncovered in 325 degree oven for one hour. Serves six, or more.

SPAGHETTI FOR A WHOLE BUNCH

4 tablespoons butter or olive oil

3 cups chopped onion

4 cloves garlic, chopped fine

2 green peppers

2 large cans mushrooms (stems and pieces)

3 bouillon cubes in 1 1/2 cups water

2 cups red wine

2 cans tomato paste

2 cans tomato sauce

2 large cans tomatoes

1 can pitted black olives (chop into halves or quarters)

2 tablespoons parsley

2 lbs. ground beef

1 lb. ground pork

2 bay leaves

season salt and season pepper

about 1/2 jar McCormick Italian seasoning

oregano

Romano and/or Parmesan cheese

In frying pan saute onion, garlic, peppers, in butter or oil. In separate pan brown meat. In big pot put in tomatoes, tomato sauce and paste, wine, mushrooms with juice, olives with juice, all herbs and seasonings. Then add meat and onions and peppers to pot.

Cover and simmer slowly day before for 2 or 3 hours — then again before serving. Add more wine or bouillon if sauce gets too thick.

Boil spaghetti in usual manner, rinse and drain. Pile on plates, top with sauce and plenty of Parmesan or Romano cheese, grated. Also serve green salad and French bread.

BERT CROSS
Aspen's portraitist — in sketch or pastels.

LOEY RINGQUIST
One of the most beautiful gardens you'll ever see is at Loey's
Faraway Ranch up Snowmass.

SLUM GULLION

Loey recommends this as a good dish to fix after a day's horseback riding
into the Colorado Rockies.

You get the campfire going and while the flames are settling down, you
pull over the cooking pannier, haul out the dutch oven, a long handled spoon,
the can opener, bacon fat and begin. Start to simmer a big fat onion or two
lean ones, cut up with one or two bell peppers (red ones in season have the
keenest flavor). Add 1½ to 2 lbs. hamburger or ground round. Stir. Then reach
into the pannier again and get one can tomatoes and 2 cans any kind of beans
— butter beans, lima beans, kidney beans. Add them to pot and seasonings like
salt and pepper, bit of sugar, garlic powder and maybe half teaspoon chili
powder.

By this time the fire is low enough to put on grate or ashes that foil covered loaf of French bread you fixed last night — sliced with butter and grated cheese or garlic salt.

To wash it all down is a good mixture called Rocky Mountain Moca. Often one finds it difficult to sleep in the high country so we always use sanka at night instead of instant coffee. Put a third of a cup of powdered milk in your cup, a teaspoon of cocoa and a teaspoon of sanka — add boiling water heated on the campfire. Coffee drinkers like more coffee flavor than cocoa and children like more cocoa with just a touch of the coffee.

Maroon Bells

Photographer Jeffrey Aaronson with two of his favorite models, Elsa Fischer on the left and Martha Fischer on the right.

Twirp Anderson plays his fiddle.

Larry MacIntyre is always the caterer for Martha and Dr. David Yocum's Catfish Fry...one of the first parties of the summer season.

Talking shop at the *Aspen Magazine* Writer's Symposium are left to right: Graphic artist Nina Merzbach, writer Andy Stone, and reporter Jane Wilson.

BOBBIE AND RICHARD WRIGHT

Dick is a building contractor and Bobbie manages his office.

HAM LOAF

  1 lb. uncooked ham — ground
  1 lb. lean pork — ground
  1 egg, well beaten
 ½ cup bread crumbs
 ½ cup cold milk
  2 tablespoons butter
     pepper

    Mix well, and bake at 300 degrees for 2 hours.

SAUCE

  2 egg yolks
 ¼ cup tomato soup
 ¼ cup vinegar
 ¼ cup butter
 ¼ cup liquid mustard
 ¼ cup sugar

    Put all ingredients in double boiler, stirring thoroughly first. Let warm, stirring occasionally. Serve over ham loaf warm. This is one of Bobbie's most used, most liked recipes, which was given to her by Heidi Howell. She has doubled it many times, for dinner parties.

Carved face on the Elks building

HEIDI "KIT" STANTON

Has a tremendous interest in photography.

BEEF A LA PERNETTE

  3 tablespoons fat or oil
  3 pounds lean stew beef, cut into 1½" cubes
  3 medium sized onions, thinly sliced
 ¼ cup cognac-brandy
  5 tablespoons flour
1½ cups well seasoned beef broth (bouillon)
  3 cups red Burgundy wine
  2 cloves garlic, peeled
     salt and pepper to taste

Heat the fat or oil in Dutch oven over high heat. Add beef, a few pieces at a time and brown on all sides. Remove and set aside. Reduce heat to medium, add onions and saute, stirring occasionally. Replace beef. Heat the cognac and flame the beef. Remove beef. Add flour to pan and stir until blended. Gradually add broth and cook, stirring constantly until thickened. Stir in the wine. Add the garlic and replace the beef. Cover and finish cooking in a preheated 325 oven for 2½ hours or until the meat is fork tender. (Discard the garlic cloves.) This is good to prepare the day before serving, refrigerate and reheat before a big party.

NICHOLAS deVORE III

An Aspen photographer, Nicholas goes out on assignment often for National Geographic Magazine.

LOST REMUDA RICE

This hearty dish is best eaten above 10,000 feet just at dusk. Serves two ravenous explorers.

Two medium size zucchini
Four slices bacon
Four ounces Philadelphia cream cheese
One Schilling mushroom gravy mix
Six ounces of Uncle Bens long grain wild rice
One ounce roasted soybeans or sunflower seeds

Add 2½ cups cold water to wild rice packets. Add diced bacon to pot and cover. Boil 20 minutes. Stir occasionally.

Add sliced zucchini and mushroom gravy mix. Stir over heat for five minutes.

Divide equally, especially bacon. Top with cream cheese and crunchy soybeans. Salt to taste.

A ⅗-ounce package of Sapporo Ichiban may be substituted for rice.

Note: Leave rice box at home and pack out what you pack in.

DON GOODWIN

Singing in the Aspen High School musical productions, Don has gone on to cutting the records, "This Is My Song" and "A Time To Cry" and has been guest artist on several TV shows.

BEEF, OLIVES or OXRULADER

8 slices beef (1¼ to 1¾ lbs.)
salt, white pepper

STUFFING
    4 ozs. butter, parsley, tangerines or two small juicy oranges.

FOR FRYING AND STEWING
    butter
    1½ cup stock or water

SAUCE
    1¼ cup gravy
    2 tablespoons of cream
    1 tablespoon plain flour
Cooking time about 1½ hours.

Pound the slices of beef lightly and sprinkle with seasoning. Mix the parsley and butter, divide among the beef slices. Put on top a section of tangerine or orange and roll up the slice. Secure each "olive" or roll with a wooden toothpick.

Heat the butter and put in the "olives." Brown them all over. Add the soup stock or water, cover with a lid and cook gently.

Dilute the gravy with water if necessary. Add cream (thicken the gravy and allow the sauce to cook for 3-5 minutes.) Taste for seasoning.

Serve with boiled or fried potatoes, boiled vegetables, a green salad and Lingonberry preserve or chutney.

PENNY ONEGIAN

She manages a restaurant for the Skiing Corporation
in Breckenridge, but spends as much time as possible in Aspen.

STUFFED GRAPE LEAVES

- 1 jar salted grape leaves, rinsed
  (if you're lucky, you may have your own vineyard)
- 1 lb. ground lamb, or beef, or a combination of both
- 1 medium onion, finely chopped
- ¾ cup rice, parboiled
- 1 tablespoon chopped fresh parsley
- ¼ cup pine nuts (optional)
  salt, pepper to taste
- 2 cloves of coarsly chopped garlic

Mix lamb or beef, onion, rice, nuts and seasonings together. Mixture should be slightly moist. If too dry, add a little liquid (water, broth or tomato sauce).

Open one grape leaf on your palm, shiny side down, and place about 1 tablespoon of the meat mixture on the top third. Fold over the top and the two sides and roll into a sausage shape. Do not roll too tightly.

Arrange in a casserole in layers. Scatter the garlic between layers and on top. Pour enough liquid to cover. Place a flat plate over the stuffed grape leaves so that they do not move. Cook on top of the stove (or in the oven, medium heat) until thoroughly cooked (about one hour or so in Aspen). Can be served both hot or cold with yogurt or lemon.

BARBARA GAZARIAN McLOUGHLIN

She has a red caboose shop, located on The Pride of Aspen Mine Dump, where she custom makes skating outfits for Aspen ice skaters.

OLD WORLD ARMENIAN SHISHKABOB

  1 leg of lamb, cubed (1½" cubes)
1½ cups chopped onion
  4 or 5 cloves garlic, slivered
  2 cups catsup mixed with
  3 or 4 tablespoons worcestershire
Ample salt and pepper
Sprinkle generously with allspice
Sprinkle with wine vinegar

Mix lamb and spices thoroughly. Cover tightly and let marinate for several hours, preferably overnight.

Alternate meat cubes with small whole onions, green pepper and mushrooms on skewers.

Cook SLOWLY over charcoal turning often for about an hour. Do not cook well done. Delicious with rice pilaff.

Aspen gables

JERRY HILL

An Indian trader, Jerry travels to the pueblos of New Mexico and Arizona collecting old pawn pieces, hishi, silver and turquoise, which he brings back to trade or sell to the shops in Aspen.

BUCKAROO STEW

Jerry learned this recipe from an old cowboy from Sonora that he worked for.

1 to 2 medium sized potatoes per person
2 strips of bacon per person
½ onion per person

Slice potatoes in quarters, slice onions or chop in pieces, to size you prefer. Chop raw bacon in 1 inch strips.

Boil over open fire in large cast iron pot or in large skillet adding water until potatoes break down into mush. Serve like home fries for breakfast on the trail. Guaranteed to warm your gizzard.

KURT WIGGER

Kurt Wigger was the chef many years for Werner Kuster's Red Onion Restaurant in Aspen and now he has his own places, called Sopris Restaurant, near Carbondale and Buffalo Valley in Glenwood.

BEEF STROGANOFF

2 tbs butter
1 lb lean fillet of beef cubed
1 tbs chopped onion
1 tbs chopped fresh parsley
salt, pepper, Paprika and
    Accent to taste
1 jigger French brandy

1 tbs butter
½ cup fresh tomato, diced
6 fresh mushrooms
1 minced dill pickle
2 jiggers red wine
8 tbs brown gravy
2 tbs sour cream
dash of heavy cream

Melt butter in heavy skillet until bubbling. Add meat, saute 2 minutes for medium rare. Add onion, parsley, salt, pepper, Paprika and Accent, saute another 20 seconds. Flame with brandy. Remove from heat. Put meat in a warm dish.

Heat pan, add butter, tomato, mushrooms and pickles. Saute, stir in wine and brown gravy, cook until bubbling.

Add meat and cook together for 10 seconds. Add sour cream and heavy cream. Stir, serve with noodles and vegetable garnish. Serves two.

JAN SARPA'S BEEF ON NOODLES

The following recipe serves 8, is elegant, yet simple and can be prepared ahead of time for ease of serving. Makes a nice winter meal with a salad.

    2 lbs lean beef (I use filet,
        quality of meat is important!)
  ¼ cup butter
    1 chopped onion
    1 large can mushroom slices
juice of 1 lemon
    2 tablespoons flour
  ½ cup beef boullion
salt and pepper to taste
  ½ cup sour cream
    3 tablespoons sherry

first: saute beef with onion until browned, can set aside (refrigerate) until time to serve and then add sliced mushrooms, sour cream, beef boullion, sherry, salt and pepper. Serve hot over broad egg noodles. I prepare noodles right before serving the dish and "dress" the noodles with heated butter and beef boullion to taste.

JAN JONES SARPA

A former model, Jan Jones Sarpa is now an Aspen psychologist.

The Aspen social seasons are filled with dances, including country western dances.

MEAT LOAF

2 eggs, slightly beaten
1 package dry onion soup
1½ to 2 lbs chopped beef
⅛ lb chopped pork
1 cup bread crumbs
1 cup sour cream

Mix ingredients together with one tablespoon cold water.

Bake in loaf pan at 350 to 375 degrees for one hour.

Pour off fat and serve.

MERRILL FORD

The Aspen Institute is one of Merrill's passions. This sculpture was produced by Herbert Bayer for the Institute in the 1950s. Years later, in the 1990s, Merrill discovered it stored in a garage and had it restored and returned to its place on the grounds of The Aspen Meadows. The photo of Herbert Bayer is courtesy of the Aluminum Company of America.

TINGA POBLANA

    2 lbs rump or skirt of beef

    1 small can chile verde (green chile) in strips

    1 lb tomatoes (Roma)

    1 small can of tomato paste

    ½ lb tomatillo verde (green)

    1 onion medium size

    3 Chorizo sausages

chile chipotle to taste

Cook the meat in the pressure cooker with thyme, bay leaf, marjoram.

When ready leave it to cool and then separate.

Reserve one cup of broth, the rest is to use in this recipe.

Put the Chorizo sausage without the skin to fry on a 10" skillet, then add the onion in pieces.

Meanwhile put the broth to boil with tomatoes and tomatillos. When ready, liquefy. If using chipotle, put in now.

Add the meat to the skillet with Chorizo and onion and add tomato mix and chile verde, let them cook again for 30 minutes to blend in flavors.

Serve with white rice and/or refried beans.

Good to make burritos with or to top tostadas.

MAVISA RODRIGUEZ GARZA

Mavisa Rodriguez Garza always comes to the *Food & Wine Magazine* Aspen Classic. Her family has a winery in Mexico and they also have a home in Aspen.

Crater Lake above Maroon Lake.

ROBERT'S GOURMET SOURBRATEN

Served with Basil Polenta

Sourbraten: Beef should marinade for 4 to 5 days

One whole beef tenderloin, season with salt and pepper

 3 cups red wine

 ½ cup red wine vinegar

 6 bay leaves

 1 cup diced yellow onion

 1 cup diced carrots

 1 cup diced celery

 5 whole cloves of garlic

marinade should completely cover beef

Preparation:

2 quarts of beef stock

corn starch

4 mushrooms of choice, sauteed

parsley

Remove beef from marinade and hard sear on all sides.

Transfer marinade to a non-reactive saucepot and bring to a boil.

Remove foam and discard. Strain marinade and add to beef stock.

Adding beef at this time and bring to boil, reduce and simmer for 1½ hours.

Thicken with cornstarch as needed and garnish with mushrooms and parsley.

Basil Polenta:

½ up whole milk

½ cup heavy cream

1 cup water

3 oz polenta, fine grain

2 tablespoons of julienne of fresh basil

¾ oz basil butter

salt and pepper

Preparation:

Combine first three ingredients and bring to boil, stir in polenta and cook for about 10 minutes on low heat until soft, stirring constantly. Add the remaining ingredients. Salt and pepper to taste. Serve immediately.

ROBERT SUTER

Robert Suter owns European Caterers and he creates fabulous meals for many Aspen parties.

ITALIAN MEATBALLS

1 pound ground beef

2 beaten eggs

1 clove garlic, minced

1 small onion, minced

2 tablespoons parsley, minced

¼ cup grated fresh parmesan cheese

½ teaspoon salt

2 cans tomato paste

3 cans hot water (use cans from tomato paste)

1 teaspoon dried sweet basil

½ teaspoon salt, ½ teaspoon freshly ground pepper, ½ teaspoon sugar

Mix together (with wet hands) ground beef, eggs, garlic, onion, parsley, cheese and salt.

Form into about 16 balls (they'll be soft, but that's ok).

In a skillet, combine tomato paste, hot water, basil, and other seasonings; mix well; bring to a simmer.

Drop meat balls into the sauce, slowly; cover and simmer for about one hour.

Serve over pasta with more freshly-grated parmesan cheese and a good Chianti Classico or Valpolicella wine.

MARIE TACHE

Marie and Yvan Tache have raised a family of ski racers in Aspen. They are, left to right: Chris Tache, Michelle Scott, Mark and Christin Tache, Yvan and Marie Tache, Danielle Tache Irons, and Michael Tache. They are all great skiers.

SPAGHETTI

½ medium onion, chopped

2 cloves garlic, minced

1 green pepper, chopped

one 8-oz. can tomato sauce

one 8-oz. can mushrooms (stems and pieces)

one 28-oz. can whole tomatoes

1 pound ground beef

Lawrey's season salt, pepper, garlic powder

1 package Lawrey's spaghetti sauce seasonings (no substitute)

Brown meat, pour off grease. Add tomatoes, tomato sauce, season salt, pepper, garlic powder. Cover and simmer 30 minutes. Add Lawrey's spaghetti sauce mix, onions, garlic, green pepper, mushrooms. Simmer 30 minutes. Stir occasionally.

Boil spaghetti, rinse and drain. Pile on plates, top with sauce and grated parmesan or romano cheese. Serve with green salad and French bread.

If you have lots of boys (like Marie), double this recipe.

An Aspen Victorian decorated for the Christmas season.

LASAGNE

Here are some comments by Barbara on her very popular lasagne recipe:

"This is one of the dishes our daughter Cindy and her husband Drake Jacobs wanted served to their wedding party. When our son and daughter, Greg and Jennifer Gomon, are home, I try to send them off with frozen servings in paper bowls secured in zip-locked bags, ready for the microwave.

This is also the recipe that many of the Home Economics students requested during my 13 years at Aspen High School, and they are still requesting it.

Ingredients:

1 pound sweet Italian sausage
1 pound extra lean ground beef
½ cup finely chopped onion
2 cloves garlic, crushed
1 tablespoon sugar
1 tablespoon dried basil leaves
½ teaspoon fennel seed
1 teaspoon salt
1 can (2 pounds, 3 oz.) Italian-style tomatoes
1 can (15 oz.) tomato sauce
1 can (6 oz.) tomato paste

1 cup water

10 oz. curly lasagne noodles

2 eggs

3 cups fresh Ricotta cheese

½ cup fresh grated Parmesan cheese

½ cup fresh chopped parsley, packed

½ teaspoon salt

½ teaspoon pepper

1½ pounds fresh whole milk or skim milk mozzarella cheese in water, sliced very thin

Directions:

Remove outer casing from Italian sausage. Saute sausage, ground beef, onion and garlic in 5-quart Dutch oven until browned, about 25 minutes. Brown slowly and stir frequently. Place mixture in collander, press, and drain excess fat.

Add next 8 ingredients. Break tomatoes up with fork. Bring to boiling; reduce heat; simmer, covered and stirring occasionally, about one hour or until mixture is the consistency of spaghetti sauce.

Cook lasagne noodles in large amount of boiling salted water to which 1 tablespoon of olive oil is added. Cook only until tender; drain in collander; rinse under cold water. Dry lasagne on paper towels.

Preheat oven to 375 degrees F.

Beat eggs; add next 6 ingredients, and beat until completely mixed. Do not add the mozzarella yet.

Layer half the noodles in a 14" x 11½" x 2¼" deep baking dish; spread with half the Ricotta filling; half the mozzarella cheese, and half the meat sauce. Repeat.

Bake at 375 degrees about 30 minutes (or assemble early and refrigerate; then bake about 45 minutes).

For easier cutting, let stand 15 minutes after removing from oven.

Serves 12 to 15 persons.

BARBARA SHULL-JORDAN

Barbara and her husband, Marv Jordan, own and operate the Timberline Book and Poster Shop on the Hyman Ave. Mall. Barbara was also head of the home economics department for many years at Aspen High School. With her students and townspeople she put on an annual Christmas arts and crafts fair for many years.

PORK ROAST

    about 5 pounds of pork roast tied together
carrots, as many as you want to use (cut up)
5 tomatoes
3 onions
2 dinner spoons of oil
2 teaspoons butter
spices: thyme, laurel, oregano, salt and pepper

First stir the oil and butter in a baking dish. Put the pork roast in the oven at 500 degrees and let it brown on both sides.

When it is browned, lower heat to 350 degrees. Add the onions and carrots. After 15 minutes, stir vegetables around and add tomatoes. Cook for 2 hours.

Add water if tomatoes have not given enough juice.

When serving, slice on a nice platter. Put carrots around, onions and tomatoes should be used as decorations on platter.

CHRISTINE AUBALE—GERSCHEL

Christine founded Les Dames de Ballet which later evolved into Les Dames d'Aspen, a group of ladies who put on parties and gala dances that benefit the arts groups in Aspen.

Willam Christensen, who brought ballet to Aspen, is flanked by students of the Dance Aspen summer dance school.

STEIN ERIKSEN

Stein is the golden man of skiing...first winning Olympic gold medals, then keeping the flame of skiing going through all the years.

FAAR I KAAL
(LAMB IN CABBAGE STEW)

Big pot — First one layer of cut-up cabbage...cover bottom of pot. Then one layer of lamb meat, cut up in small ½-squares. Some fat on the meat makes better flavor. Any meat from lamb is good; some rib pieces improve flavor.

Then sprinkle ground pepper and salt on layer of meat. Repeat...cabbage, meat, salt and pepper until finished, layer after layer.

When done, add water, about ½ inch from bottom. In the morning, bring to boil, simmer the rest of the day. Stir frequently. Serve with boiled potatoes.

TONY VAGNEUR
Tony grew up on the Vagneur Ranch in Woody Creek. He often plays his accordian at old-timer parties.

MOUNTAIN STEW

Ingredients: 2¼ lbs. beef stew meat, 3 beef neck bones, 3 large carrots, 5 stalks celery, 4 good size potatoes, ½ pound brussel sprouts (more or less), ½ pound of mushrooms, 2 green bell peppers, 2 large onions, 3 or 4 cups of beef stock, and a couple bouillon cubes. Also, 1 bay leaf, some dill weed, tarragon, oregano, rosemary, 2 cloves of garlic, and some worcestershire sauce. Carrots should be sliced, celery the same. Cut potatoes into good sized chunks, do the same with the onions, and slice up the bell peppers. Use the rest whole.

To cook: Begin by simmering the neck bones and 2 cups of beef stock for about 25 minutes. This should be a light simmer so the beef stock doesn't boil away. Use a lid. Then add half of bay leaf, the carrots and the stew meat. Put in the pot one diced clove of garlic and 4 or 5 shakes out of the worcestershire sauce bottle. Simmer this about 20 more minutes, adding a little pepper if you like it. Next, add the celery, a small pinch of dill weed, and a pinch each of tarragon and oregano. Also add about 5 needles of rosemary. At this point, you may need to add a couple more cups of beef stock. You can substitute beef bouillon and water. Add this whenever you need to. Keep on simmering for another 15 minutes or so, adding another 4 or 5 shakes out of the worcestershire bottle along the way. No sense to get in a hurry. Now, add the brussel sprouts (or lima beans if you prefer) and simmer again for about 10 minutes. Better taste it now. You should be getting very hungry and the stew should be very tasty. Throw in the potatoes and the other diced clove of garlic. Add some more pepper and worcestershire sauce, but go light this time. Wait about 15 minutes and then add the green peppers, which should cook for about 10 minutes. During the last few minutes, add the mushrooms. They need very little cooking time. Done! Just take your time and enjoy cooking this stew. The world will wait because this is the most important thing you're doing right now.

GERTA WALLS

Gerta lives in Aspen half of the year and in her home city of Vienna, Austria the other half. She is an art restorer and brings back to original beauty many an art piece.

HUNGARIAN (VIENNESE) GOULASH

3 pounds beef chuck

3 pounds onions

2 green peppers

2 cloves garlic

2 tablespoons caraway seeds

1½ teaspoon granulated sugar

½ teaspoon freshly ground black pepper

5 tablespoons (or more) imported paprika

1½ tablespoons salt

1½ sticks butter or fat, some bacon drippings

Cut meat in cubes, brown in part of the butter. Saute onions in rest of butter, fat and bacon drippings until light golden, mix together with the browned meat, put seasoning over it. Cover with water or beef stock, slice the green peppers, put everything in heavy skillet and simmer for 1½ hours or until meat is tender. Thicken sauce with flour or corn starch.

Serve with noodles, spaetzle, or boiled potatoes.

Serves 6 people.

GAEL GREENE

Novelist, author of **Blue Skies, No Candy** and **Dr Love**, and restaurant critic for **New York** magazine, Gael lives in Aspen whenever she can get away from New York City. She says her Potluck Frittata is a dish that glorifies whatever you have left over in the fridge.

POTLUCK FRITTATA

Gael says she improvises with whatever she has on hand...doing this dish on a houseboat exploring Lake Powell left no other option. But here's the version she put together for a potluck supper in Aspen's Brand Building, in the apartment of Harley Baldwin.

1½ lb. new potatoes, boiled till tender (about 20 minutes), then drained, skinned and sliced into ¼-inch rounds

2 large red peppers, singed over the range or under the broiler to remove their skins, then cut into narrow strips or squares.

1 large red onion sliced very thin and broken into rings

2 cloves garlic, minced

salami or kielbasa, sliced thin, enough to cover the bottom of Gael's skillet (12" across the top, 2½ inch sloping sides)

4 tablespoons olive oil

10-12 large eggs at room temperature

fresh cracked pepper, fresh grated parmesan, fresh chopped herbs or parsley

Heat 2 tablespoons olive oil in non-stick skillet and toss potatoes till lightly browned.

Remove potatoes, add 1 tablespoon olive oil, cook red onions till soft, then raise heat slightly and brown them lightly.

Remove and set aside. Add half a tablespoon of olive oil and toss red peppers and garlic. Cover bottom of pan with salami or kielbasa and brown on both sides, shaking to keep things from sticking.

Meanwhile, beat eggs with a fork or whisk, add lots of pepper, even hot pepper flakes if you wish. Return potatoes, red peppers, onions and garlic to pan.

Pour eggs over. Move pan frequently to keep eggs from sticking...stir eggs from bottom trying not to dislodge sausage pattern (though no one will care if you do). When eggs start to set, sprinkle with grated parmesan and set under broiler for a minute till cheese browns and top of the frittata sets.

Sprinkle with chopped parsley, cilantro, or what fresh herbs you have and serve 6 for brunch, 12 at a buffet. Gael also serves this often at room temperature brushed with a mustardy vinaigrette before sprinkling with chopped herbs.

GAARD MOSES

Gaard is a graphic artist and has painted many of the signs around Aspen. The painting of the Silver Queen statue on the side of the Brand Building is a work of art.

HOT CHILI STEW

2 tablespoons oil

7 pork chops diced to ¾'' cubes (feed bones to dogs)

1 tablespoon garlic salt (garlic powder for those of us with high blood pressure)

3 cloves chopped garlic (good for high blood pressure)

three 7-oz. cans of chopped green chilis (not jalapeno chilis)

1 large can of canned tomatoes, chopped up somewhat

1 small can tomato paste

1 can corn nuggets (not that mush stuff)

5 oz. Velveta cheese (optional)

cayenne (red pepper) to taste (at least 1 teaspoon)

½ bunch chopped cilantro (optional for Gringos)

1 finely chopped onion

2 pinches basil

Saute/fry pork in oil, salting down with garlic salt and chopped garlic.

Dump the crispy pork and garlic into large pot and add the rest of the ingredients. (Don't measure the ingredients so people will think you're a chili cook.)

Yield is 4 to 6 bowls.

Serving suggestion: Serve with tortillas and butter and Mexican beer.

TERIYAKI

Francis shares his Teriyaki recipe, a composite of many Hawaiian recipes, and the only one he knows using white wine instead of red.

Top sirloin 1 ¼ to 1 ½ inches thick. Get one pound per person, as it is wonderful sliced thin cold for lunch if any leftover.

Marinade:

1 pressed garlic clove
2 tablespoons ground ginger
2 tablespoons honey
2 tablespoons vinegar
½ cup soy sauce
½ cup white wine

Marinade for two hours, turn every half hour, poke meat with fork and baste with marinade each turn.

Broil one inch from very hot coals, seven and a half to nine minutes each side. Francis turns only once, his timing is good, but he turns when the juice starts to come to the surface. Then turn and baste with marinade for the remaining time.

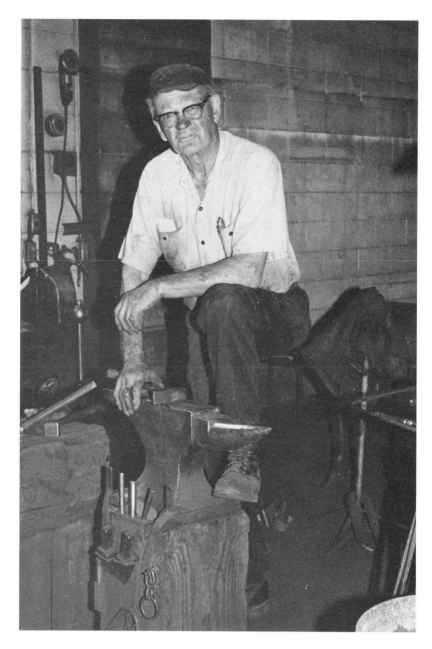

FRANCIS WHITAKER

For many years, Francis had his Forge blacksmithing workshop in Aspen. He has moved it to Carbondale where it is now part of the Colorado Rocky Mountain School. Francis was for many years a member of the Aspen City Council and a staunch supporter of Open Space.

232

SAM CAUDILL

Aspen architect Sam Caudill looks like the original Mountain Man, always garbed in his Western hat, denims and cowboy shirts. However, as a Scotsman, descended from Daniel Boone, Sam can also play a mean bagpipe.

PUMICE CREEK SUNRISE
(GOOD MORNING...ALASKA)

Take one-quarter pound of moose tenderloin, cut into one-half-inch nuggets.

Saute in butter for ten minutes, add garlic salt and lemon pepper.

Fry two eggs in butter, slowly, turn eggs "over easy," add garlic salt and lemon butter.

Warm large whole wheat tortilla.

Place fried eggs and moose nuggets on tortilla, add chopped onions, jalapeno peppers, green chile peppers and salsa.

Fold over tortilla, tighten your safety belt and serve with a shot of Yukon Jack...chased with a tumbler of "Workhorse Red," Sonoma County, Cabernet Sauvignon. Produced by Bellerose Vineyard in Dry Creek Valley, California. Or any other good Cabernet Sauvignon.

Elk or venison may be substituted for moose.

Serves one person.

AMERICAN HOT DOG

Ingredients:

Two slices of Wonder Bread

Two jumbo hot dogs

A couple thick crispy iceberg lettuce hunks

Approximately 2½ heaping tablespoons of Best Foods Real Mayonnaise

An equal amount of Heinz 57 Catsup

Two dill pickles (medium size Vlasic)

Directions:

Slap mayonnaise generously on both sides of bread. Slice hot dogs from end to end down the center and fry slowly in real butter (lightly salted) until gold brown to black on one side.

Quickly shake generous amount of catsup over mayonnaise and smudge into mayo with index finger. You may choose to lick finger to test the balance of catsup to mayonnaise. Carefully place pickle slices on what you will determine as the bottom slice of bread. Apply catsup over pickle slices. Then place sizzling hot dogs on bottom half and add lettuce and top piece of bread.

Earl recommends cutting sandwich in half, dissecting hot dogs.

He says this insures easier handling and also enables consumer to manipulate sandwich in a graceful manner while holding a glass of ice cold chocolate milk in the other hand...which further enhances this culinary delight. Use 3 heaping teaspoons of Nestles Quick in a glass of Vitamin D milk.

EARL BISS

Earl is one of the famous young contemporary American Indian artists who were trained at the American Indian Art Institute in Santa Fe. These artists have made a name for themselves throughout the Southwest and the world. Earl has lived in Aspen on and off for the past 15 years. He is well represented in Aspen art galleries.

234

DAN GLIDDEN

Also known as Luke Short, Jr., Dan is writing Western novels in much the same style as his father, famed writer of Western novels Luke Short (Fred Glidden). Dan works in a studio in the Seven Castles area of the Frying Pan River. He writes of cowboys and Indians, buttes and washes, of everything about the Old West.

POJOAQUE CHILI RELLENOS

This recipe is from years past when the families of Fred Glidden, Jon Glidden and Francis Kalmes gathered for a chili-making party. Today, whenever possible Dan and wife, Sharon, and their five daughters drive to. Pojoaque in early fall to purchase a bushel of chilis just a quarter mile from the old Glidden home. Dan was raised in Pojoaque, New Mexico and Aspen, Colorado, and is a mixture of both cultures.

fresh green chilis
3 to 4 eggs
1 to 1½ cups milk
4 or more cups flour
cheddar or jack cheese, cut into strips
oil for deep frying

Beat eggs well. Add milk. Stir. Mix in flour until smooth. Batter should be thick enough to coat the chilis.

Prepare the chilis by washing, cutting tops off, and removing the seeds. Gently scrape the seeds out. (A long-handled infant spoon works well.) Stuff cheese strips into the chilis. Dip one at a time into the batter for a light coating. Deep fry three or four at a time until golden brown. Turn only once. Make more batter as needed.

These freeze well and can be reheated for impressive hors d'oeuvres or a quick meal in a microwave or conventional oven.

JANE DUNBAR

Jane is one of those Aspenites with whom we became friends when her children and our children were all growing up here together. Even when we were both pregnant and she struggling with painting and myself struggling with photography ... she always found time to pose for my camera.

VERY EASY PARTY HAM

Jane says she first had this party ham at the home of a Cuban friend, Mercedes Cassidy, in Palm Beach.

Thereafter whenever Jane wanted to serve it she had to call Mercedes who in turn would phone the Cuban grocery in West Palm Beach and in Spanish order it from the butcher. They spoke no English. However it was always ready for Jane when she went to pick it up.

When she moved back to Aspen, Jane had to concoct her own sauce to resemble, as closely as possible, the Cuban sauce.

She says it is great to take to potluck dinners, Blue Lady lunches, picnics at West Buttermilk Ski Area, picnics in the wilds during the summer, or serve at cocktail parties.

Have butcher slice thinly a whole or half boneless ham and tie together loosely with string.

Mix together to make a paste: 1 cup dark brown sugar, powdered mustard, cinnamon, nutmeg, ground cloves to taste. Moisten with undiluted frozen orange juice. Stir in lots of cracked black pepper. Spread this glop all over top and sides of ham. Put in 400 degree pre-heated oven for about 45 minutes to 1 hour. Place thin orange slices on top for last 20 minutes or so.

During cooking glop more goo on ham or baste with melted drippings. If ham is fat or has lots of water, you might want to drain off some drippings before serving.

Cut string to allow sauce to get between slices if butcher has tied ham too tightly.

Jane serves this ham with party pumpernickel or rye bread and perhaps some horseradish if one wants it even hotter to taste.

The John P. Marquand house was made of three Aspen Victorian cottages all joined together. Wild roses bloomed outside. Jane Dunbar and her husband, Chuck Dunbar, and their children lived here for several years.

TOM MUNN

Tom is Aspen's cowboy poet. He recites his poetry and sings his songs at Cowboy Poet meetings around the West. He is also a real cowboy.

TOM MUNN'S COW CAMP CHILE

Note: Because of the high altitude of most Rocky Mountain cow camps, use canned chile beans. This meal can be served, from start to finish, in ½ hour.

Cut up 4 green peppers.

Cut up 2 onions.

Cook slowly in greased frying pan.

In a separate frying pan, cook 1 pound ground meat (beef, wapiti, venison).

In a large saucepan, add 2 cups water, 2 large cans Kuners chili beans in sauce, chili pepper is included.

1 large can stewed tomatoes

1 small can tomato puree

Let cook 15 minutes, then add, after draining, the peppers, onions, and meat. Serve four hungry cowboys.

If you want the chili soupy, add 2 cups water.

OLD LEFTY'S WILL
© 1975 by Tom Munn

Old Lefty died a cowboy
The only life he ever knew
And he left all he had to his lovin' wife
Though his possessions numbered few
But his will contained the strangest thing
The lawyers ever read
Cause when they opened his last testament: This is what it said.

Chorus:
Now honey when I die ya'll skin me out
And go ahead and tan my hide
And make me into a saddle
So I'll be there for you to ride
Then I'll always be right in between
The two things that I love
With my horse ridin' down below me
And my woman up above.

Don't take me to be crazy
I still control my faculties.
You can bury my bones
But save my hide now honey won't you please.
Then I'll always be a cowboy
Still ride around the range
Darlin' do this last thing for me
Even though it sounds so strange.

Repeat chorus.

CELEBRITIES

Many celebrities come to Aspen but this group all own homes in Aspen.

Kevin Costner and Paula Zahn were stars at the 50th Anniversary party for the Aspen Music Festival in 1999.

Mike and Marian Peters love to attend the Food & Wine Classic in Aspen. Mike is a Pulitzer Prize winning editorial cartoonist and he also does the daily cartoon, "Mother Goose and Grimm."

Goldie Hawn and Ivana Trump waited for their cues during a benefit for the Tibetan people held in Aspen.

Burt Bacharach gave a concert in Aspen for the Sunshine Kids (kids who are suffering from cancer). The Bishop family gave a dinner before the concert. Left to right are Sandie Bishop, Allison Holmes, Burt Bacharach, Thompson Bishop, Mo Mullen and Archer Bishop Jr.

JILL AND LEON URIS

Jill is a photographer and Leon is a novelist. Together they produced **Ireland, A Terrible Beauty** with Jill's photographs and Leon's prose. Leon is the author of **Exodus, Trinity,** and the **Haj, Battle Cry** among others.

BRAISED LAMB SHANKS

6 lamb shanks	1 cup dry red wine
¼ cup flour	1 cup beef broth
salt	1 cup water
pepper	2 13-oz. cans tomatoes
½ cup olive oil	½ teaspoon marjoram
3 medium onions, coarsely chopped	½ teaspoon rosemary
3 ribs celery, coarsely chopped	1 bay leaf
2 cloves garlic, minced	1 teaspoon curry
1 green pepper, minced	

Preheat oven to 325 degrees. Sprinkle lamb shanks with salt and pepper and flour. Heat ¼ cup oil in heavy skillet and brown shanks. While shanks are browning, saute onion and garlic in remaining oil in large casserole until transparent. Add green pepper and celery and cook 5 minutes. Add wine, broth, tomatoes and herbs and bring to a boil. Arrange shanks on top of vegetable mix and spoon sauce over meat. Cover and cook for two and a half to three hours or until meat is very tender. Spoon off fat. Serve over noodles. Serves six.

ENCHILADAS

1 can (28 ounces) Las Palmas chili sauce

4 tablespoons flour

2 cups water

dash of salt

1 dozen corn tortillas

½ pound longhorn cheese, grated

½ cup chopped onion

1 can roast beef or stew meat cooked to the stringy stage

Brown flour slightly, add Red Chili Las Palmas, stir until smooth, add water and cook until thick. Dip tortilla in warm sauce. Take out as soon as soft, put on a plate, add small portion of onion, cheese and beef. Fold or roll. Repeat until all tortillas are filled and rolled. Cover with sauce and heat in 350 degree oven for 30 minutes.

You may substitute either red or green enchilada sauce and omit the water.

MARION BYRNE—GETZ

Marion owns the Byrne-Getz Gallery which specializes in Southwestern art and jewelry. Growing up in Yuma, Arizona, she is an authority on Southwest artists and their work, traveling directly to the American Indian reservations and foundries to obtain the work. Here she talks to an artist at the Shidoni Foundry in Tesuque.

F I S H

BAKED TROUT

Place cleaned trout on foil — wrap individually. Dot trout with butter, salt and pepper, several onion rings. Pour over 2 tablespoons dry white wine and lemon juice if desired.

Wrap tightly in the foil and bake in a hot oven for 15 to 20 minutes (depending on the size of the fish). Small trout recommended.

JOYCE McDONALD
At the Chamber of Commerce.

Old stage road over Independence Pass.

KATIE LEE
Folk singer and lover of wilderness areas — she has written songs about the Colorado River.

COLLARDS AFRICANS

In frying pan melt 1 cube margarine in which you saute 2 packages frozen (or equal amount of fresh) collard greens. Saute just enough to melt and warm. Add 2 cans of smoked oysters, squeeze in juice of quarter section of lemon, salt and pepper to taste. Add about ½ cup white wine or Champagne, simmer for 20 minutes.

Note: Original recipe used a green from Africa and collard greens are the closest. If you live in the East, smoked whitefish can be used instead of oysters.

MARIELLEN POWERS
A marvelous secretary.

ALMOND CRAB CASSEROLE

1 cup crab meat
1 cup cleaned shrimp
2 cans mushroom soup
1 cup chopped celery
¼ cup minced onions
2 three oz. cans Chinese noodles
1 package shaved almonds
¼ cup Sherry

Combine all ingredients in a buttered casserole, except noodles and almonds. Refrigerate overnight or several hours. Add noodles and mix and sprinkle almonds on top before putting in oven. Bake at 375 degrees for 30 minutes or until bubbly. Excellent for brunch or buffet dinner. Serve with green salad and French bread.

MARY MIKELL WARHURST

When friends come back we picnic them — here's Mary with the Lanes and Hayes and her Jamie — she used to own the Aspen Bookshop and is now a nurse in Vermont.

SHRIMP GUMBO

This is Mary's great-grandmother's recipe, from Charleston, S.C. Saute 2 slices bacon, dice it or use 2 tablespoons bacon fat. Add 1 can okra (or 1 lb. fresh okra). Drain canned okra well.

2 minced onions	2 stalks diced celery
1 small green pepper, minced	1 #2 can tomatoes
Blend in 2 tablespoons flour	1 bay leaf
Add 3 cups meat stock	1 teaspoon Worcestershire sauce
(or canned consomme)	

Simmer, covered, for 1 hour.

Then add shrimp — I use at least two cans. Can also use veal or chicken. Salt and pepper. Cook for 5 minutes longer and serve over rice. You can make this up ahead of time and keep on warm, if you have an electric saucepan or deep pot — until ready to serve and then add the shrimp.

HJORDIS SKAERINGSSON

Hjordis Skaeringsson came to Aspen from Iceland and she and her husband, Ulfar, raised their family here.

Hjordis worked many years for Terese David in her boutique and Aslaug often was a model for children's clothes.

ARTICHOKE SHRIMP LINGUINE

Aslaug's mother, Hjordis, always let her help in the kitchen, and this is one of the recipes she taught her.

1 lb large shrimp
1 pkg linguine
2 to 3 cloves garlic, minced
½ stick butter
½ cup olive oil
2 cups marinated artichoke hearts (drained)
pinch red pepper flakes
¼ cup pine nuts
½ cup golden raisins
1 cup fresh chopped basil
1 tbs dried parsley
Parmesan cheese

1. melt butter, add olive oil, pepper flakes, raisins, pine nuts, basil, garlic, and artichokes
2. saute two to three minutes
3. put in shrimp and cook covered for two to three minutes
4. toss with cooked linguine and fresh Parmesan cheese, sprinkle with chopped parsley

Steps 1-3 can be done ahead

DIANE AND TONY RUTGERS

Tony and Diane Rutgers. Tony is an Aspen contractor and Diane owns Pyramid Travel. They spend time in Tahiti as Tony's grandfather was James Norman Hall, who with Charles Nordhoff, wrote the classic novels about the South Pacific, "Mutiny on the Bounty," "Men Against the Sea," and "Pitcairn's Island."

TAHITIAN STYLE SHRIMP CURRY

2 lbs medium sized shrimp — peeled and washed

3 large red tomatoes

1 bunch cilantro

2 bunches green onions

1 can "Lite" Thai Coconut Milk
(available at Clark's Market)

½ cup white wine

½ cup sour cream

1½ cans chicken broth

olive oil and 1 tablespoon butter to saute

garlic salt to taste

3 tablespoons of curry-or to taste

Saute onions until golden — add cilantro and tomatoes. Use garlic salt at this time — add curry to taste.

Add the white wine and saute again. Add the coconut milk-to make it a sauce-like mixture.

Saute shrimp in another pan-until just cooked.

Add the shrimp to the mixture — then add the chicken broth.

Let simmer for 1 hour — very low.

Just before serving turn up heat and add sour cream at the end.

Sauce should be medium thick. Taste and correct for seasoning.

Use a small amount of cornstarch if mixture needs thickening.

Serve over white rice with chutney.

Condiments: chopped peanuts, raisins, chopped bananas

ERIC CALDERON

Eric Calderon is the manager of The Little Nell Hotel. He's also a great dancer.

ERIC'S BBQ SALMON

serves 6-8

Ingredients

1 side of salmon

2 onions, thinly sliced

lemon juice

Dressing Ingredients

½ cup olive oil

¼ cup Worchester sauce

½ cup soy sauce

¼ cup honey

½ teaspoon ground ginger

Cooking Instructions

Spread half the onions on tin foil. Lay the salmon on the onions, cover with the remaining onions. In a bowl mix dressing and pour over the salmon. Wrap the salmon with the tin foil. BBQ for about 20 minutes at medium-high temperature.

BAKED SALMON

4 to 5 lbs. fresh or frozen salmon thawed overnight and marinated in milk several hours.

Make a sauce of:

1 cup white wine
5 to 6 teaspoons butter
⅛ teaspoon dill weed
   white pepper and salt to taste
½ teaspoon mustard
½ to 1 tablespoon parsley
2 teaspoons lemon juice
1 teaspoon shallots, chopped fine.

Melt butter, add wine and spices, add lemon juice and onion and simmer for 20 minutes.

Drain salmon and dry with paper towel. Heavily season with lemon herb garni and lemon pepper and some salt.

Spread 2 teaspoons butter on double foil, and slices of lemon on bottom. Place salmon in foil and pour over with the sauce, and lemon slices on top. Seal foil and bake for 1½ hours at 350 degrees.

TOM SARDY

A Pitkin County Commissioner for some 30 years, Tom was also longtime owner of Aspen Lumber and Supply, commonly known as Sardy's. He is the first in Aspen to rake his lawn every Spring.

CHARLES DALE

Charles Dale is the owner and chef at Renaissance and Rustique Restaurants in Aspen. He grew up in the royal palace of Monaco as his father was private advisor to Prince Rainier on the economic affairs of Monaco. Charles has earned many honors and awards as a chef.

SLOW-ROASTED SALMON BRUSCHETTA

Serves four

The salmon marinade is based on the traditional Scandinavian method of curing called "graavlax." Charles played with the cultural affinities by substituting oregano for dill, and a lemon-flavored vodka and Pernod for the traditional aquavit. He says he cures the fish only long enough (three hours as opposed to twenty-four) for it to disgorge some of its water content, thus yielding a slightly crisp outer surface, and a deliciously moist interior texture by virtue of the slow roasting process. Tomato, arugula, capers and Parmesan cheese round out the Mediterranean flavors.

Time saver tip: start the tomatoes as soon as they are seeded and chopped; add the other ingredients later.

4 fresh salmon filets (not steaks), approximately 6 oz each, skin on

Zest of ½ lemon, chopped

3 tablespoons coarse salt, preferably kosher

2 tablespoons raw sugar

1 tablespoon chopped fresh oregano

2 tablespoons Absolut Citron

2 tablespoons Metaxa Ouzo or Pernod

Tomato Jam

6 large, ripe tomatoes, peeled, seeded, and
  chopped

2 cloves garlic, chopped

¼ cup red wine vinegar

¼ cup sugar

pinch salt

4 slices (½ inch thick) hearty country bread

Arugula Salad

¼ pound fresh arugula

⅓ cup extra virgin olive oil

1 lemon, juiced

2 tablespoons large nonpareil capers

¼ pound Reggiano Parmesan cheese,
  in one piece

Mix together the salt, sugar, oregano, lemon zest, vodka and ouzo or Pernod. Pour into a plastic or stainless steel container, and place the salmon filets skin side up on top of the mixture. Cover tightly and refrigerate for two to three hours.

Meanwhile make the tomato jam: add all the ingredients in a small, non-corrosive saucepan, and simmer gently for two hours. Keep warm until ready to serve.

Preheat the oven to 220 degrees.

Place the four salmon filets, skin side down, on an un-greased baking sheet; do not remove the marinade from the surface of the salmon. Slowly roast the salmon filets for 15 to 20 minutes, or until they just begin to split when gently squeezed.

Brush the sliced bread with extra virgin olive oil, and toast it in the oven. In a medium bowl, toss the arugula with the lemon juice, olive oil, and capers. Shave the parmesan cheese into the salad with the aid of a potato peeler, or the large holes on a metal grater.

To Serve

Remove the salmon from the baking sheet by pulling it off the skin with a pair of tongs; alternatively, you may use a spatula, but be sure to leave the skin attached to the baking sheet.

Place a small dollop of the tomato jam in the center of four plates, put a slice of bread on top, and spread a healthy portion of the tomato jam on each piece of bread. Stack the cooked salmon on top of this, then top again with the arugula salad. Serve immediately.

Charles and his wife, Aimee, often cook up a fabulous meal for friends at home.

CHRIS CASSATT

Chris Cassatt has been a resident of Aspen since 1970. He worked with Potpourri author Mary Eshbaugh Hayes at The Aspen Times for more than 15 years. He is author of the internationally syndicated comic strip 'Shoe.' He also, with partner Gary Brookins, illustrates humor columnist Dave Barry's column.

NUGGETS BY CHRIS CASSATT

Colorado home-grown Hors-doeuvres.

Check to see that you have a current Colorado fishing license.

Brookies cannot be purchased in a store. You have to catch them.

They live in high mountain streams rather than rivers. In the Aspen area they can be found in Hunter Creek, Lincoln Creek, Lost Man, and the Frying Pan above Ruedi.

You'll need to catch a mess of Brookies — at least 4 per person.

They range in size from about 6 to 10 inches.

Brookies are not really trout. They are a Char and are related to the Arctic Char.

They differ from Rainbow and other river trout in several ways. They have no scales on their skin and their meat can be pale gold to almost salmon red depending on their diet.

Ingredients:

Brookies

flour

raw eggs

Progresso Italian-seasoned breadcrumbs

course-ground pepper

peanut oil

fresh lemon.

Preparation:

After rinsing the Brookies in water, fillet them, leaving the skin on. Since they can be fairly small, I recommend a small, extremely sharp fillet knife — 5 or 6-inch blade.

Once filleted, cut into chunks about an inch to an inch and a half.

Breadcrumb/flour mixture: On a large plate place a cup or more of breadcrumbs and mix in several tablespoons of flour and some course-ground pepper.

Dip fillet pieces in beaten raw egg then coat with breadcrumb/flour mixture.

Flash fry these pieces in peanut oil on medium high heat until they start to turn golden. This usually only takes a minute or two. Note: the skin of the fillet starts to bubble away from the meat indicating the fish is cooked. Don't overcook.

Remove nuggets from oil and drain on paper towels. Sprinkle with salt and pepper, then squeeze fresh lemon juice over them and serve.

SUD DOWS

Sud Dows and his wife, Judy, lived in Aspen many years and were staunch supporters of the arts community...in fact they endowed the Dows Barn for the Anderson Ranch Arts Center. Sud also was a ski instructor at Aspen Highlands Ski Area. They are now living back in their home state of Iowa and spending summers at their lake cabin in Wisconsin.

OPEN—FACE SHRIMP SANDWICH (for two)

    1 can small shrimp rinsed and drained
    1 can (small) sliced pineapple drained
    2 slices Swiss cheese
    2 slices whole wheat bread, toasted
    1 cup sauce (below)
    Sauce:
    ½ cup mayonnaise
    1 tablespoon Dijon mustard or to taste
    1 teaspoon lemon juice or to taste
    Mix sauce well.

Place shrimp, mixed with sauce on toast. Cover with one slice of pineapple, then with cheese. Broil until cheese is melted and pineapple and shrimp are hot. Serve at once.

Sud says this is great for a last minute winter lunch. He has also made this recipe for large groups with a green salad on the side.

FAST RICE, SCALLOP, VEGETABLE DINNER FOR CASUAL ENTERTAINING

Ingredients (for 2 to 3 persons):

1 pound scallops

¾ pound mushrooms

3 (1 each) red, yellow and green peppers

1 onion

2-3 green long onions

1 small gresh ginger root

1 dash vegetable salt

a few turns of pepper mill

1 clove garlic (optional)

¼ of a fresh lemon

few twigs parsley

3 tablespoons safflower oil or olive oil

2-3 cups rice

Preparation:

1. Cook well-washed rice preferably in Oriental electric rice boiler.

2. Sprinkle some lemon juice over scallops.

3. Heat choice of oil in pan and simmer scallops slowly for about 5 minutes (addition of minced garlic optional).

4. Grate fresh ginger root, then use squeezed juice only over the scallops.

5. Add sliced mushrooms and finely cut red, yellow and green peppers.

6. Add vegetable salt and freshly ground pepper.

7. Add 1 tablespoon of white wine.

Let all ingredients simmer for about four minutes uncovered. According to preference, this dish can be served either in the center of a rice-ring or: the rice can be carefully blended with the mixture in the pan and then served. Sprinkle minced parsley over the dish before serving.

TAMARA MERZBACH

A photographer and creator of jewelry. Her home-studio is just outside Carbondale with a fantastic view of Mount Sopris.

BOB AND KAY SIMMONS

Bob and Kay are each famous for their special talents. Kay is an expert horse rider, she competes in. . . and wins in many Western horse shows. Bob is an avid fisherman both summer and winter. They both are famous for this smoked trout recipe. Once, they were even flown to Australia to teach the recipe to a restaurant owner and his staff.

During the late 1950's Kay and Bob would keep a ladder leaned against the house, so they could smoke fish and chicken on top of the chimney. They used a four-sided wooden frame covered with chicken wire.

The idea was to build a **small** smokey fire in the fireplace with aspen wood and they would climb up and down the ladder to check the doneness. With wine and cheese: Excellent!

They would have neighborhood get-togethers for these parties. Everyone would bring something and there were those who would have it at their houses and only furnish the electricity. Great fun in a simpler time.

Bob catches real Trout. . . Bates Hayes makes them in silver.

KAY SIMMONS

MODERN ASPEN SMOKED TROUT

1. Obtain an electric "Little Chief" Smoker, which has three small stainless racks, a hot plate, and a frying pan for holding chips.

2. Plug in the smoker and fill the frying pan with chips, bark, or pieces of aspen, hickory, or apple wood. It will smoke heavily in about 15 to 20 minutes.

3. Take the rack out of the smoker and place the fish on the three racks. 9 small trout is about right. Holding the fish in your hand, **pour** salt from box of salt in the cavity and then liberally on both sides. Place fish on the racks, with the largest fish on the bottom.

4. Check smoke each hour; adding bark, etc. as needed. You might have to empty the chips pan once.

5. Cook for three hours. Remove from smoke.

6. Wash off fish with running water.

7. Check with fork for doneness. If it is a little raw for your taste, put in microwave about one minute per fish for small fish and two minutes per fish for medium fish.

8. **Bone.** Put on plate with crackers and lemon.

9. Enjoy! You'll wish you had more.

Note: Bob says he doesn't kill stream trout, and you shouldn't either. Use stocker fish from reservoirs, Clark's or City Market.

DIANE EAGLE—KATAOKA
A radio personality and writer, Diane also does great
historical research.

PAN BARBEQUED SHRIMP

16 tablespoons unsalted butter

3 or 4 garlic cloves, minced

½ teaspoon fresh rosemary leaves, crushed

½ teaspoon dried oregano

1 teaspoon cayenne pepper

1 bay leaf, crushed

½ teaspoon freshly ground black pepper

4 thyme sprigs, chopped, or ½ teaspoon dried thyme

salt to taste

2 pounds unshelled large or jumbo shrimp, rinsed briefly in cold water

½ cup bottled clam juice

¼ cup dry white wine

1. In a large frying pan, melt half the butter over high heat. Add the garlic and herbs. Stir well and add the shrimp. Cook about three minutes, stirring and shaking the pan.

2. Add remaining 8 tablespoons of butter, clam juice and wine. Cook, stirring and shaking the pan, for three more minutes. Remove from heat and serve immediately with the hot butter from the pan. Serve with side dish of spaghetti and marinara sauce, French bread, salad.

Four servings.

FOOD & WINE MAGAZINE CLASSIC AT ASPEN

Talking under the big tent are, left to right: famous chef Jacques Pepin, publicist Jan Fox and W. Peter Prestcott who first got the magazine involved in the Aspen Food & Wine fest.

Every summer, thousands of people come from all over the world to eat and drink at the *Food & Wine Magazine* Classic in Aspen.

Gary Plumley founded the first Wine Festival in Aspen.

Debbie Fields (Mrs. Field's Cookies), on the left, talks to Terry Vitale, publisher of *Colorado Expressions Magazine*.

Annette Shafer pours some wine for Aspen film writer Tracy Wynn.

ROCKY MOUNTAIN TROUT

From Woods Lake Days

Trout-clean, (slice open in cleaning), leave bone in, head on.

Roll in cornmeal, fry lightly in bacon grease, serve whole.

Serve with:

Broiled tomatoes, topped with bread crumbs seasoned with onions and parsley.

Pan fried potatoes, sliced crosswise.

CUCUMBER SALAD

Peel and slice cucumbers crosswise, peel and slice white onions (red ok), marinate in cider vinegar and ground pepper. Chill in ice. (Today I'm sure you could use gourmet vinegar and vary the onions).

Dessert at Woods Lake would have been homemade vanilla ice cream from their own cows which children of guests were allowed to milk.

At Woods Lake, the Bowles family (the resort owners) smoked small trout over willow smoke (the lake was a private resort so the small ones were legal). We used them as hors d'oeuvres all winter.

MARY GARDNER

Mary Gardner grew up in Colorado Springs and when she was a young girl, her family always vacationed at Woods Lake, up the Frying Pan River. Now an Aspenite, Mary worked at the front desk for many years at *The Aspen Times*.

The Aspen Times staff are great party goers. Mary and Gib Gardner at a picnic where one of the Times dogs is interested in their goodies

TOM MOSSBRUCKER AND JEAN PHILIPPE MALATY

Jean Philippe Malaty is the Executive Director of Aspen/Santa Fe Ballet Company and School and Tom Mossbrucker is the Artistic Director. They both danced professionally, Tom with the Joffrey Ballet where he performed principal roles in over 70 ballets. He teaches tap and ballet with the school. Jean Philippe has performed soloist ballet roles with various companies throughout the country including Joffrey II, Los Angeles Classical Ballet, and Ballet Hispanico of New York. He teaches ballet with the school.

Jean Philippe was the director of the first "Nutty Nutcracker" for Aspen Ballet and he encourages Stascha Kaelin who was the Sugar Plum Fairy.

JEAN PHILIPPE'S CREPES

Makes about 12 crepes 8" diameter

4 eggs

3 cups flour

1 quart liquid: 2 cups water

                   2 cups milk

1 cup granulated sugar

1 teaspoon vanilla extract

1 dash salt

1 teaspoon oil

In a mixing bowl, put dry ingredients, make a well and add eggs, oil and vanilla extract. Mix with wood spatula. Slowly add liquid till getting a smooth soft consistency, but not too runny. You can always add more liquid later. Let sit at least an hour, mixture will get thicker.

Over medium heat, in a buttered skillet or non-stick frying pan, pour a ladleful of batter evenly. Let cook until edges start getting color, then flip over and cook other side for a minute or two. Spread about two tablespoons of flavoring on top of crepe and roll it.

Flavoring

1 cup lemon orange rind grated

1 cup granulated sugar

½ tablespoon rum

TOM'S BISCOTTI

These are great after dinner with coffee

  ¾ cup whole almonds
  ¼ pound butter
  ¾ cup sugar
  2 eggs
zest from 1 orange grated
  2 tablespoons Irish Whisky
  1 teaspoon cinnamon
2¼ cups flour
1½ teaspoons baking powder
  ¼ teaspoon salt
  ½ cup toffee bits

Preheat the oven to 350 degrees. Toast almonds until light golden and chop into chunks. Reduce heat to 325. Cream butter and sugar. Add eggs and beat until smooth. Mix in orange zest, whisky and cinnamon. Mix in flour, baking powder and salt and beat just until mixed. Stir in chopped almonds and toffee bits. On a lightly floured board, divide the dough in half and form each half into a long roll about 8 to 10 inches long. Bake on nonstick baking sheet in the top third of the oven for about 25 minutes or until lightly browned on top. Remove from oven and let cool for 10 to 15 minutes. Slice on the diagonal about ½ inch thick. Lay the slices flat on the cookie sheet and bake for 10 minutes. Turn biscotti over and bake another 10 minutes. Let cool and stand for several hours before eating.

Tom leads his tap class.

Bebe Schweppe is the founder of Aspen Ballet and one year she danced the part of the Sugar Plum Fairy in the Nutty Nutcracker.

BETTY WEISS

A patron of the arts in Aspen, Betty Weiss is also a talented painter, exhibiting in Aspen art galleries. She pours tea at the Tea on the Terrace for the Aspen Music Festival. Ruth Winters is behind her.

ALMOND CRESCENTS

1 cup butter

2 cups flour

½ pound almonds, blanched and chopped fine

2 tablespoons powdered sugar

2 cups powdered sugar for rolling

Cream butter, add dry ingredients. Shape into crescents and bake on ungreased cookie sheet about 10 minutes at 400 degrees. Roll in sugar, cool and roll again.

Betty is also a great supporter of the Aspen/Santa Fe Ballet and enjoyed the can can executed by the ballerinas during the Moulin Rouge party.

FRESH STRAWBERRY PIE

Easy and delicious, Bonnie is well known for this pie.

1 quart strawberries
1 cup sugar
2 tablespoons cornstarch
1 baked pastry shell
1 cup whipping cream

Mash one pint of strawberries until juice is well extracted, bring to a boil, add sugar mixed with cornstarch, and cook until clear and thick. Place 1 pint of whole berries in the baked pastry shell. Pour over these the hot cooked berries, and then place in refrigerator until very cold. Top with sweetened whipped cream before serving.

BONNIE MCCLOSKEY

Bonnie McCloskey helped found the Roaring Fork Chapter of the Colorado Women's Foundation which encourages girls and women to be all they can be and promotes the "full participation of women and girls in society."

BLUEBERRY CAKE WITH CARAMEL SAUCE

¾ cup sugar

⅓ cup butter

Cream butter and sugar

add 1 egg

1 cup flour

1¼ teaspoon baking powder

½ cup milk

pinch salt

Add 1½ cup blueberries, floured

Bake at 350 degrees

Caramel Sauce

1½ cup brown sugar

1 cup water

⅓ cup butter

vanilla

1 teaspoon cornstarch

cook until thickens

Pour sauce over cake and serve hot with vanilla ice cream

ANN NITZE

Ann Nitze is an elegant hostess in both Aspen and Washington, D.C.

Ann and her husband, Bill Nitze, dance at the gala for the opening of the Aspen Music Festival's Harris Hall in 1993.

MARY ANN HYDE

Mary Ann Hyde gives one of the most fabulous Christmas parties in Aspen.

PECAN PIE

    1 unbaked pie shell
    3 lightly beaten eggs
    ¾ cup corn syrup
    ¾ cup sugar (white)
    ¼ teaspoon salt
    3 tablespoons melted butter
    2 teaspoons vanilla
    1 cup pecan pieces

Mix eggs and syrup well. Stir in sugar, salt, melted butter and vanilla and blend. Let stand 5 minutes and pour into unbaked pie shell. Sprinkle pecan pieces on top. Bake at 350 degrees for 40 minutes. I add a dollop of whipped cream when serving and don't count the calories.

When the new Aspen Music Tent was dedicated, Aspenites thronged to look it over.

JUDY GREENE HAAS

Aspen artist Judy Greene Haas is famous for her paintings of Rocky Mountain Trout.

CREAM CHEESE PIE

Graham Cracker Crust:

1 stick butter

10 graham crackers (turned into crumbs)

⅓ cup finely chopped pecans

2 TBS maple syrup

Melt butter. Combine all ingredients together in a bowl. Press and pat the crumb mixture into the pie pan.

Filling: Preheat oven to 350 degrees

2 large cream cheese

2¼ tsp vanilla

2 eggs

⅔ cup sugar

Blend and pour ingredients into the graham cracker crust. Bake at 350 degrees for 20 minutes. Let cool 5 minutes.

Topping:

1 cup sour cream

2 TBS sugar

1 tsp vanilla

Blend the above ingredients. Pour on top of the cooling pie and bake another 10 minutes. Refrigerate pie for 2 hours.

MARIA ALLENDE'S FLAN

A — 1 cup of sugar (to do the caramel for the mold)

B — 5 eggs

1 can evaporated milk without diluting

1 teaspoon vanilla

1¼ cup sugar

1 — Preheat oven to 350 degrees F

2 — Use a rectangular bread loaf mold and put it on the stove at medium heat with 1 cup sugar to caramelize the mold all around. It should be aluminum 6" deep by 8" long or a round one of 8" diameter. Keep melting the sugar until it takes a light golden color. Be sure to spread the caramel all around the sides of the mold all the way to ½" from top.

3 — On the side, in a bowl put the 5 eggs and all the rest of ingredients in B. Mix them all and strain them into the caramelized mold. You can strain them into another bowl and then pour them in the mold.

4 — Get a bigger mold with very hot water and put the caramelized mold with the ingredients inside this mold with water. This is called "Bano Maria" (Maria's Bath).

5 — Put like this in the oven for 1 hour 15 minutes or until you see it a golden color.

6 — Take out of the oven and of the pan with the water. Let it sit to cool down. As soon as you can, put it in the refrige, cover it and put in the refrige until ready to serve.

7 — To serve, put it upside down onto a platter so the caramel drips down.

Enjoy!

MARIA AND FERNANDO ALLENDE

Fernando and Maria Allende. Fernando is a famous Latin singer and movie star and Maria is his manager. While living in Aspen many years, Fernando often gave concerts to benefit the Aspen Education Foundation.

PATTY DE FRIES
Now at The Peppermint Tree.

Community Church

ENGLISH TOFFEE

½ lb. butter
  1 cup sugar
½ cup chopped pecans
  3 small plain chocolate Hershey bars

   Combine butter and sugar and cook over medium high heat, stirring constantly. If mixture separates, lower heat until it combines again. Cook until a light brown taffy color. Pour and spread in 9 x 9 pan, which has been covered with ⅓ cup of pecans. Immediately put chocolate bars on top and spread over candy as it melts. Sprinkle remaining nuts on top and cool.

MARY BARBEE
She originated the Peppermint Tree Candy Shop in Aspen.

LOLLYPOPS

2 cups sugar   1 cup water
⅔ cup light corn syrup   flavoring and coloring

Put sugar, corn syrup and water in pan and cook, stirring only 'til sugar is dissolved. Continue cooking, without stirring until the stage — very brittle in cold water — is reached. During cooking, wipe the sides of pan with wet cloth to remove sugar crystals. Pour out on marble slab and stick lollypop sticks into each.

Frosting to decorate lollypops with: ½ box confectioners (powdered) sugar, lump of butter, ¼ teaspoon cream of tartar — cream well.

GREAT-GRANPA'S TAFFY

2 cups white sugar
1 cup brown Karo syrup
2 tablespoons vinegar
2 tablespoons butter

Boil until it will crack in water. Add ½ teaspoon soda. Pour on buttered platter. When cool, pull until light-colored and cut with shears.

PAULI HAYES
Takes this taffy to her school and church parties. She's wearing a hat made from Jean Knight's recipe — page 36.

At Durant mine.

MARGOT DICK
One summer afternoon Margot made us this cake from her grandmother's recipe.

APRICOT UPSIDE-DOWN CAKE

1 stick butter
1 cup brown sugar
  package of pecans

1 can apricot halves in heavy syrup
  (No. 2½ can or 3½ cups)
1 yellow cake mix

Melt butter slightly in heavy frying pan. Spread evenly over this the brown sugar, the apricots — hollow side up, and the pecans. Mix cake batter as directed on box, using apricot juice for liquid instead of water. Pour cake batter over the sugar, apricots and pecans. Bake in frying pan. When done, turn over onto platter — apricots up.

NANCY ALLEN
Free time is spent in riding her horse "Saroya" in the Woody Creek area.

OATMEAL COOKIES

    1 cup butter

    1 cup white sugar

    1 cup brown sugar

    2 eggs

    1 teaspoon soda

½ teaspoon salt

    1 teaspoon vanilla

1¾ cup flour

    3 cups oatmeal

    Mix in order given. If mixer is used, stir oatmeal in last, by hand. Walnuts optional. Lemon flavoring may be substituted for the vanilla.

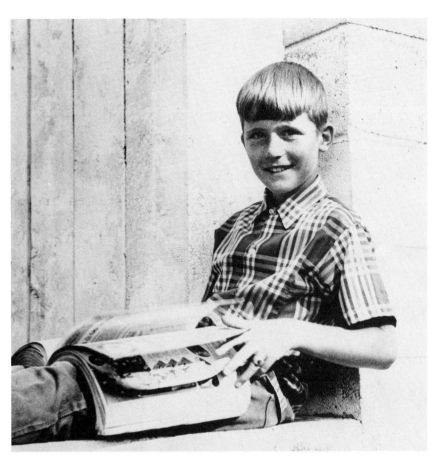

MARK DAY
The boy next door.

SUGAR COOKIES

1 cup shortening	½ teaspoon salt
1 cup sugar	1½ teaspoon vanilla
2 eggs	2½ cups flour
	1 teaspoon baking powder

Cream sugar and shortening, add eggs, then rest of ingredients. Chill. Roll out and cut with fancy cookie cutters. Frost with different colors of confectioners sugar frosting — made with box of confectioners sugar, butter the size of a walnut, vanilla, cream or milk to spreading consistency. Dust with sugar. These make the best Christmas cookies, or special cookies for any occasion.

RUSSIAN CREME

1 cup granulated sugar

2 egg yolks

2 tablespoons brandy or pineapple juice

2 egg whites

1 small carton whipping cream

Stir egg yolks for 10 minutes. Mix sugar with egg yolks. Put in ice box to chill.

Beat egg whites stiff, add 2 tablespoons brandy or pineapple juice. Gradually add egg whites and whipped cream into yellow mixture. Serve.

A. O. FORBES

A. O. has a "big sound" band and it plays for many of the school dances.

Playing at the eighth grade graduation dance.

ANN TAYLOR
The Arrow Shop is the Taylor's Aspen venture.

STRAWBERRY ICEBOX PIE (Makes two 9-inch pies)

1 large can evaporated milk

1 package strawberry jello

1 cup hot water

1 can or package frozen sliced strawberries

Chill milk, and whip until the consistency of whipped cream. Dissolve jello in water and add to frozen strawberries. Pour this mixture into the whipped milk and stir until well dissolved.

Pour into pie shells (either pastry crust or graham cracker crust) and place in refrigerator for several hours before serving.

GRAHAM CRACKER CRUST (Makes 2 crusts)

1 stick of butter or margarine

½ cup sugar

2 cups graham cracker crumbs

Grease two pie plates. Soften stick of margarine. Mix sugar with crumbs, then add softened margarine. Mix thoroughly and pour into pie plates. Crust is now ready or may be chilled before adding filling.

CAROL HOLLARS
Teaching swimming during the summer recreational program.

CHOCOLATE PECAN PIE in Meringue Shell

2 egg whites   ⅛ teaspoon salt   ⅛ teaspoon cream tartar

Beat until foamy — add gradually ½ cup sifted sugar and beat well until very stiff, almost dry. Fold in ½ cup finely chopped pecans and ½ teaspoon vanilla. Spread in greased 8" pie pan — ½" above pan. Bake in slow oven (300 degrees) for 50 to 55 minutes. Cool. Melt 1 package (4 oz.) German sweet chocolate in 3 tablespoons water over low heat, stirring constantly. Cool 'til thickened and add 1 teaspoon vanilla. Fold in 1 cup whipped cream and spread in pie shell. Cool about 2 hours.

KATIE LEWIS
Another crucible digger.

CHOCOLATE MOCHA PIE FILLING

Katie gave me the same recipe for the Chocolate Pecan Pie in Meringue shell — but she varies the pie filling somewhat. Use same meringue pie shell as Carol's recipe — try this filling.

4 oz. sweet chocolate

3 tablespoons strong black coffee

1 teaspoon vanilla

1 cup heavy cream, whipped

Put chocolate, coffee, in saucepan over low flame. When smooth, stir in vanilla. Cool, then fold in whipped cream, turn into shell. Cool 2 hours.

July's red poppy.

JULIE STRICKLAND

Niece of Aspen teachers Mona Frost and Lucille Price, Julie works at Sports Obermeyer.

FROZEN LEMON PIE

This recipe is from her grandmother, "Honey" Robison.

3 egg yolks	½ teaspoon grated lemon rind
⅛ teaspoon salt	3 egg whites
½ cup sugar	1 cup cream (whipped)
¼ cup lemon juice	¾ cup crushed vanilla wafers

Beat egg yolks, salt and sugar in top of double boiler. Stir in lemon juice and rind and cook over hot, **not** boiling, water until mixture thickens and coats spoon.

Remove from stove and chill.

Beat egg whites until stiff and then fold in whipped cream and cooked mixture.

Sprinkle half of the wafer crumbs in freezing tray, then pour in mixture. Top with remaining crumbs and cool until firm. Serve in finger length slices.

EDITH ALBERTA BOWLBY
Renovator of many Aspen Victorians.

Staircase in the old Tom Beck home —
owned at one time by Mrs. Bowlby.

APPLESAUCE CAKE

  1 cup butter (or substitute)
  2 cups sugar
  3 eggs
  2 cups applesauce (unsweetened)
  2 teaspoons soda
  4 cups flour
  1 teaspoon cinnamon
  1 teaspoon cloves
  1 teaspoon salt
½ teaspoon ginger

    Cream butter and add sugar and beaten eggs.
Mix applesauce and soda, add to creamed mixture.
Sift flour and spices — add to mixture. Add 1 cup
raisins and 1 cup broken pecan nut meats. Place
some pecan halves over top of cake batter before
baking. Lightly grease and flour angel food cake pan
and bake for 1 hour at 350 degrees.

RENATE BRAUN
Former Pitkin County librarian — for ten years.

LINGER TORTE

½ lb. butter	1 teaspoon grated lemon rind
1 cup sugar	2 cups flour
2 egg yolks	1 teaspoon cinnamon
1 cup unblanched almonds, ground	½ teaspoon ground cloves
	raspberry or apricot preserves

Cream butter and sugar well. Add egg yolks and beat well. Stir in almonds and lemon rind. Sift together flour, cinnamon and cloves and fold into creamed mixture. Knead until dough is firm and holds together. Pat ⅔ of dough into 9" round cake pan. Layer should be ½" thick. Spread with preserves. Form eight ½" thick strips with the rest of the dough and make a lattice top, using four strips one way and four the other. Bake 30 to 40 minutes. Cut into pie shaped pieces.

TERESA M. BIRLAUF

Ladies all over Aspen serve Gugelhupf for tea — from this recipe they got from Mrs. Birlauf.

GUGELHUPF (A German coffee cake)

½ cup sugar

½ cup butter (or margarine or half and half)

2 eggs well beaten together with the above.

Then add

½ cup warm milk

½ cup warm water

1 cake yeast (dissolved in the warm water with ½ teaspoon sugar)

grated rind of one lemon

4 cups of flour

Knead well, let rise until double. Form dough — use well greased Gugelhupf form if you have one — or regular bread pan. Bake at 345 degrees about half hour. When cool, sprinkle with powdered sugar.

BRANDIED PEACHES

Select ripe, firm Colorado peaches from Aspen's Farmers Market. Rub away the fuzz with a coarse towel.

Make a syrup of equal parts sugar and water (allow 1 cup sugar and 1 cup water for each pound of fruit) in a heavy saucepan. Simmer until the sugar dissolves and the syrup is thick.

Simmer the peaches in the syrup for 5 minutes. Drain and place the peaches in sterile jars. Pour over each jar 2 to 4 tablespoons of brandy.

Pour the syrup over the fruit, filling the jars. Seal and process in a boiling-water bath (see "Joy of Cooking") for 30 minutes. Store in a cool dark place for three months before using.

Sara suggests serving the brandied peaches as a dessert...chilled with heavy, whipped or ice cream. They are also delicious served as an accompaniment with roasted meat or poultry.

SARA GARTON

Sara Garton has been the longtime proofreader at The Aspen Times. She also serves on the Planning and Zoning Commission.

VIOLET LAVEY
One of the picnickingest people I know — she and her friends like to take, for just an hour or two, whatever they have in the house and go lunch in the woods.

CHOCOLATE CAKE

½ cup sugar   1 cup milk   3 tablespoons cocoa

    Cook until slightly thickened.

    Cream 1 cup sugar into ½ cup shortening and mix well together with ½ cup milk, 2 eggs and 2 cups flour. Then add the above cooked cocoa mixture.

    Lastly add 1 teaspoon soda in 3 tablespoons boiling water. Bake at 350 degrees.

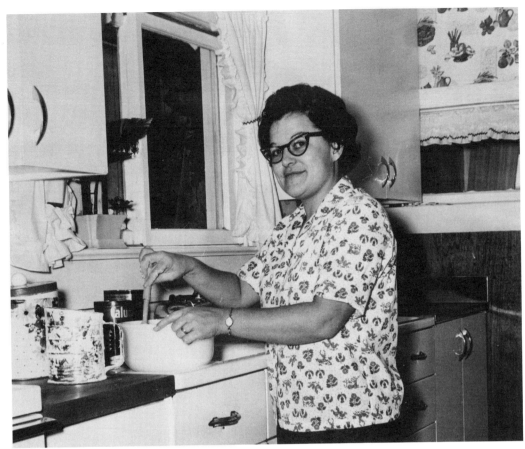

EMMA LOU TACKER
Likes to bake this cake for family occasions.

HIGH ALTITUDE CHOCOLATE CAKE (3 layers)

2¼ cups flour

¾ teaspoon soda

¾ teaspoon baking powder

½ teaspoon salt

1½ teaspoon vanilla

6 tablespoons shortening

1¼ cups sugar

3 eggs

1⅛ cups milk

⅓ cup hot water

⅓ cup cocoa

Sift flour once, then measure and mix with soda, baking powder and salt. Cream shortening and add sugar gradually, add vanilla, then well beaten eggs (one at a time). Beat in flour mixture, alternating with milk. Mix cocoa and hot water to form paste, add to batter. Bake at 350 degrees for 25 to 30 minutes in 3 layer pans.

NEVER FAIL CHOCOLATE CAKE

1½ cups flour
  1 cup sugar
  2 tablespoons cocoa
½ teaspoon salt
  Mix together and make a "well" in the center.
  Into the well put:
  1 egg   ½ cup oil
½ teaspoon vanilla

Over this pour 1 teaspoon baking soda, dissolved in 1 cup hot water. Mix well. Grease and flour an 8" x 8" pan. Bake at 350 degrees for about 45 minutes. Cool and sprinkle with powdered sugar. This recipe can be doubled or tripled.

SARAH JURICK
She designs and makes children's clothes.

GEORGIA BISHOP AND ETHEL FROST

These two friends have worked years and years together at local elections, Georgie as clerk and Ethel as judge.

GEORGIA'S WHIPPED CREAM CAKE

4 eggs (whole eggs)	¼ teaspoon salt
1 cup sugar	1 teaspoon vanilla
1½ cup sifted cake flour	1 teaspoon almond
½ teaspoon baking powder	1 cup (½-pint) cream, whipped

Beat eggs until very light, gradually beat in sugar. Fold in flour, baking powder and salt sifted together. Add flavorings and fold in whipped cream. Put in two greased cake pans, bake at 350 degrees for 25 minutes or until cake springs back from sides of pan. Georgie always makes a "try cake" in a small pan before she bakes the large cake — then she can adjust.

ETHEL'S COFFEE CAKE

Mix in this order:

¾ of a cube of butter	3 eggs
1 cup sugar	1 cup raisins
½ cup molasses or corn syrup	flour to make a stiff batter
1 pkg. mince meat, dissolved in cup of coffee	1 teaspoon baking soda, dissolved in a little water, at last.

Makes two bread pans.

GEORGINA GRONNER

A vivacious redhead.

PETITS FOURS

Mix 6 egg yolks with 6 heaping tablespoons sugar and six flat tablespoons flour, add 6 beaten egg whites. Spread on buttered paper on a baking sheet about ½ to ¾-inch thick. Bake in 300 degree oven until mixture no longer sticks to paper (about 20 minutes). Put another sheet of paper over mixture and roll up while hot from both sides, which makes two rolls. When cool, slice through the center and remove all paper. One roll is filled with chocolate cream and frosted with coffee icing, the other is filled with coffee cream and covered with chocolate icing.* When rolls have been filled and iced, slice each roll into approximately 15 pieces and put into little paper cups.

*Chocolate cream — 1 stick of sweet unsalted butter, 2 egg yolks, 6 oz. bittersweet chocolate (melted), little whisky.

Coffee cream — 1 stick of unsalted butter well beaten. Powder sugar to taste, 2 egg yolks thickened over the fire with 4 tablespoons of strong coffee, add to butter and beat well. Add little rum.

Chocolate frosting — slowly heat 6 oz. semi-sweet chocolate with 3 oz. unsalted butter. Spread when cool.

Coffee frosting — mix enough sugar into one beaten egg white, so you may spread it, add some dissolved instant coffee and a tablespoon of rum.

VIVIENNE JONES

You'll meet Vivienne at the Aspen Highlands Ski Area.

CHOCOLATE NUT FUDGE

⅔ cup evaporated milk

1⅔ cups white sugar

Cook milk and sugar 5 minutes, stirring constantly. Remove from heat and add:

1½ cups chocolate chips (or peppermint flavored chips)

1½ cups marshmallows

½ teaspoon salt

1 teaspoon vanilla

½ cup nuts

Stir all together. Pour in greased pan, sets quickly.

SALLY BARLOW

A former writer for "The Aspen Times," Sally is now free lancing.

AUNTY'S HERMIT COOKIES (recipe about 100 years old)

1 scant cup butter
2 eggs
1 teaspoon soda in sour milk
½ teaspoon salt
¼ teaspoon cloves
1½ cups sugar
5 tablespoons sour milk or sour cream
2 cups flour
1 teaspoon cinnamon
1 scant cup raisins

Cream butter and eggs and sugar. Sift flour onto waxed paper. Pour flour back into sifter and add salt and cloves and cinnamon — set aside. Mix soda with the sour milk or sour cream and add to the creamed butter mixture. Now sift flour, a little at a time, into mixture. Cream VERY well. It should be neither thick nor runny. Add raisins when it is all creamed. Bake about 350 degrees 10 minutes. Take them off cookie sheet with a pancake turner and lay on waxed paper to get crisp. Do not put in cookie jar until they are cool and crisp.

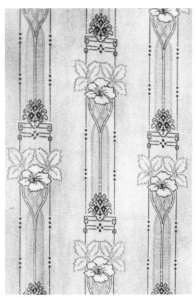

Old wallpaper.

STORMY MOHN

Not only a good lifeguard and swimming pool manager, Stormy bakes a good apple pie.

STORMY'S APPLE PIE

The secret to this recipe is the use of a full wine bottle as the rolling pin. Once wine has been disturbed that much, it should be consumed immediately and should be just about finished by the time the pie is ready.

CRUST

Mix 2 cups flour and ½ teaspoon salt, set aside. Measure ½ cup liquid salad oil and leave in measuring cup. Add 6 tablespoons milk and mix vigorously with fork so milk is suspended in oil. Immediately add mixture to flour and combine. (Like any pastry, don't overwork the dough or the crust will be tough). Divide into two equal parts and shape like fat pancakes. Instead of flouring a board, wet it and cover with a square of waxed paper. Put down a pancake and cover with another square of wax paper. Roll out with wine bottle. Take off top wax paper and put pie plate over crust, turn the whole sandwich over, remove the wax paper. Do the same for top crust (new wax paper). **Now** you can uncork the wine.

FILLING

Mix 2 teaspoons ground cinnamon, 2 tablespoons to ½ cup sugar, depending on taste, 1 tablespoon flour, set aside. Stormy's biggest complaint against frozen pies — is not enough apples. So cram as many in as possible, usually 6 or 8. Peel, core and slice apples, and when pan is about ⅓ full, sprinkle on ⅓ of cinnamon mixture, at ⅔ another ⅓ and when you finally have as many apples as you like, sprinkle on the final ⅓. Top with 6 pats of butter, put on top crust and pinch together. Cut initials of the special person you baked the pie for, or a peace sign or something for whatever mood you're in. Bake at 425 degrees for 40 minutes.

HILDUR ANDERSON

A favorite math teacher of Aspen students — Hildur is the originator of the
Mathemetiking Program given each Spring in the Middle School.

ANGEL'S DELIGHT

This recipe has come to Hildur's aid many times, when it was important
to make something for any age group-pot luck dinners, teen-age get togethers,
family dinners, picnics, a daughter-in-law serves it to her bridge club. For
smaller groups, cut the recipe in half.

1 cup milk

1 quart whipping cream

1 pound marshmallows

   crumbs of gingersnaps and vanilla wafers (or graham crackers)

Put milk in double boiler (watch very carefully if you use a pan directly
over the heat), put marshmallows in milk, watch and stir to keep from scorching.
When marshmallows have melted, set aside to cool. Whip the cream, then add
the marshmallow mixture. Pour into a large loaf pan that has the bottom
dusted with cookie crumbs. Dust the top with remaining crumbs and put in
cool place. Can be served as soon as it has set (can be set quickly in refrigerator
or deep freeze), or it can be used the next day.

GERTRUDE DENNIS' HOUSE

Now the Bruce Blakeslees'. One wintry afternoon Gertrude Dennis invited us to her little red house for gingerbread and tea — this has been one of our favorites ever since.

GINGERBREAD

2 cups flour	¼ teaspoon nutmeg
1 cup brown sugar	½ teaspoon salt
½ cup shortening	1 egg
1 teaspoon cinnamon	5 tablespoons molasses
½ teaspoon ginger	1 cup milk

½ to 1 teaspoon soda (use ½ teaspoon in Aspen as high altitude needs less)

Mix dry ingredients and shortening together, add egg, milk, molasses and soda and bake at 350 degrees. Another way, since in Aspen the brown sugar is often hard — mix flour, spices and shortening. In another bowl mix sugar with the milk, then when sugar has dissolved, add molasses and egg and then the dry ingredients, mix well and bake.

MY BEST CHEESECAKE

Thick, rich and creamy. Garnish with fresh flowers or fruit. You and your guests will love it.

CRUST

2 cups vanilla wafers
½ cup melted butter
¼ cup sugar

FILLING

5 packages cream cheese (8 oz.) softened
1 ¾ cup sugar
3 tablespoons all purpose flour
1 teaspoon grated lemon peel
1 teaspoon grated orange peel
2 tablespoons lemon juice
½ teaspoon vanilla
5 large eggs
2 large egg yolks
¼ cup heavy cream

TOPPING

¾ cup sour cream
¼ cup sugar

JOAN BRACKEN BAIN
Joan works tirelessly organizing galas that benefit Aspen's arts groups, especially DanceAspen

Combine crust ingredients in 9" springform pan and press evenly onto bottom of pan. Bake 5 minutes in preheated 375° oven. Remove and cool. Heat oven to 450°.

In large bowl beat cream cheese, sugar, flour, grated lemon and orange peels, lemon juice and vanilla till well blended. Add eggs, one at a time, and beat till well blended. Beat in heavy cream. Pour into prepared pan and bake 10 minutes. Reduce oven temperature to 300° and bake 1 hour.

Turn off oven and allow cake to remain there for one more hour. Spread sour cream and sugar mixture on top and refrigerate overnight.

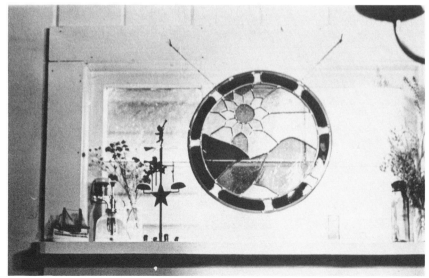

Window by Lauri LeJune Hayes.

MISSEN BRUCKER

She is one of those Aspen children you see skiing past you down the mountain.

YOGURT PIE

One graham cracker pie crust

Mix: One 8-oz. package softened cream cheese with 1 cup yogurt, 1 teaspoon vanilla and 4 to 6 tablespoons honey (to taste). Mix altogether, put into baked pie shell, chill, and serve with raspberries or strawberries on top. Is similar to a cheesecake.

Aspen Music Festival Tent

RICK ROSEN

Director and head coach of the Montezuma Basin summer ski racing school, Rick in winter ski instructs at Highlands.

CARROT CAKE

Mix together:
2 cups sifted flour
2 cups sugar
1 teaspoon soda
1 teaspoon salt
2 teaspoons or more cinnamon

Mix in 1½ cups cooking oil.
Add 4 eggs, one at a time . . . beat.
Grate and add 6 large raw carrots.
Add 1 cup chopped nuts.
Bake at 350 degrees in a low pan for about 45 minutes.

July skiing at Montezuma Basin, above Aspen.

EULA KELL

For many years Eula was a cook at Aspen Valley Hospital.

CHERRY DELIGHT

  1 cup flour (cake flour preferred)
  1 teaspoon baking powder
¼ teaspoon salt
½ cup oleo or butter
½ cup sugar
  2 eggs
  1 teaspoon vanilla
    cherries or other fruit

Beat oleo and sugar until creamy. Add eggs and beat until lemon colored. Add flour, baking powder and salt. Mix thoroughly. Add vanilla. Spread evenly on bottom of baking dish or pan, about 8 x 12-inch size. Spread cherries that have been thickened and sweetened as for pies, over dough. Bake in moderate oven about 35 minutes.

Serve with whipped topping, ice cream or just plain cream. I have used this recipe with other fruits, such as blueberries. Sliced apples with a brown sugar topping is also very good.

DR. WILLIAM COMCOWICH

An Aspen dentist, Bill is also an avid sailor, winning many races with his Day Sailer at Lake Reudi or Dillon Lake.

BREAD PUDDING

  2 cups milk plus 10 tablespoons
  4 tablespoons butter
½ teaspoon salt
½ teaspoon cinnamon
  1 cup sugar
  4 teaspoons vanilla
⅓ teaspoon nutmeg
  6 eggs
  7 ounces bread
  3 ounces raisins

     Heat milk to lukewarm, add butter and let it melt. Stir in salt, cinnamon, sugar, vanilla and nutmeg. Add raisins. Place cubed bread about ½″ size in greased 8 x 8-inch pan. Beat eggs and add to milk mixture. Pour over bread and stir around a bit. Bake in 300 degree oven for 1 hour or until it's done.

Tubing at Difficult

ALMA, BEDE and ERMA HARRIS

Whenever I need history of Hunter Creek or about the trains coming into Aspen in the "old days," I go ask Bede.

HOREHOUND CANDY

Gather horehound early in the spring.
  (A lot grows along the Rio Grande Trail
Cover leaves and stems with water.
Cook until brew is like regular tea.
Strength determines flavor.

Use: 2 cups horehound tea
      3 cups sugar
      1 teaspoon cream of tartar
      ½ teaspoon butter

Cook to 290 degrees or hard crack.
Add 1 teaspoon lemon or grapefruit
  juice at last.

  Bede's sister, Alma, uses refrigerator trays, buttered. Pour into the trays or a buttered pan, about ½-inch thick. Break into pieces.

NOTE: Catnip plant is very similar except stems are almost square. Horehound can be dried and used as a dry tea.

LEO and BOBBY BERTHOD

They live on a ranch on McLain Flats and they share their favorite Christmas recipes.

BOBBY'S WHITE FRUIT CAKE

    1 lb. margarine
    2 cups sugar
    8 eggs
    4 cups sifted flour
    2 teaspoons baking powder
    ¾ teaspoon salt
    1 lb. candied cherries
    1 lb. candied pineapple
    1 lb. pecan halves
    2 ounces lemon juice
    2 cups brandy

Preheat oven to 275 degrees. Grease and flour pans. Make two large loaves or three medium.

Soak fruit (cherries and pineapple) in 1 cup of brandy overnight.

Cream margarine and sugar. Add eggs two at a time, beating until light. Sift dry ingredients together and stir in alternately with lemon juice. Fold in fruit and nuts.

Fill pans to within one inch of top. Bake one to two hours depending on pan size. Let stand five or ten minutes, then turn out on racks to cool.

Drip 1 cup brandy on cakes until all is absorbed. Decorate with additional fruit or nuts and store, wrapped tightly in saran, then foil.

LEO'S RUM YUMMIES

    1 14 or 16 oz. package vanilla wafers rolled
        to fine crumbs
    1 cup pecans, chopped
    2 tablespoons cocoa
    1 cup powdered sugar
    2 tablespoons white Karo syrup
    ⅓ cup rum

Mix all together. Roll into small balls and roll in powdered sugar. Store in a tightly covered container. Makes about four dozen.

Elizabeth Paepcke gives a talk during ceremonies celebrating the restoration of the Hotel Jerome. Others seen in the photo are many townspeople and visitors. Bil Dunaway, publisher of the **Aspen Times**, is seated on the round couch, singer John Denver is sitting on the big couch, Robert O. Anderson, long-time head of the Aspen Institute for Humanistic Studies, is on couch at the right. The hotel reopened January, 1986.

WINE JELLY DESSERT

    juice of 2 lemons

    grated rind of one lemon

    1½ cups sugar

    1 pint ginger ale

    1 cup good Sherry (she suggests Tio Pepe)

    1½ envelope of gelatin

Put lemon juice, the grated lemon rind and the sugar with the Sherry all together and stir until melts...until the sugar is absorbed...do this in the bowl in which you will serve this dessert.

On stove have boiling water ready. Dissolve the gelatin first in ¼ cup cold water, then add ¾ cup boiling water.

Stir it into the sugar and lemon mixture.

Very last add pint of ginger ale which foams.

Stir and put in refrigerator overnight. Or if you make it in morning, put in freezer an hour or so and then into refrigerator. This is all done in a glass bowl in which you will serve the dessert.

Just before serving whip up whipping cream stiffened with sugar and vanilla. Put on top of wine jelly in little mounds.

ELIZABETH PAEPCKE

The grande dame of Aspen, Elizabeth Paepcke, and her husband, Walter Paepcke, created the present-day Aspen. They discovered the old silver-mining town of Aspen in the 1940s and led the change of Aspen into a world-famous ski resort with fabulous summer music festival. This is Mrs. Paepcke's Grandmother Nitze's recipe.

LISA CURTIS

Lisa worked in the fashion industry in New York City for many years. Now she gives workshops on how to turn stress into energy for the International Sophrology Institute. She and her husband, Curt Curtis, have an Aspen home and are always here for the skiing and part of the summer. Lisa says this recipe is from her grandmother who lived in a small Austrian village. The Night & Day Torte had been passed on for generations from mother to daughter. A torte made for special occasions, Lisa says it takes time but is worth it.

GRANDMOTHER'S NIGHT AND DAY TORTE

Night:

9 eggs

1 cup ground almonds (not blanched)

1¼ cups confectionary sugar

3¼ ribs ground Meunier chocolate (or 10 squares Maillard Bittersweet)

1 rounding tablespoon candied citron (optional)

½ stick vanilla, ground

1 pinch of baking powder

Line 9" pan with wax paper.

Heat oven.

Sift sugar with baking powder and mix with egg yolks.

Mix at least 15 min. (4 mins. with electric beater)

Add ground almonds.

Then add ground chocolate, chopped citron.

Then add ground vanilla.

Beat egg whites with a pinch of salt until stiff.

Fold in gently with pastry blender or fork.

Bake at 350 degrees for 45 mins. or until toothpick comes out clean.

Day:

6 egg whites, beaten until stiff

2½ cups confectionary sugar

2¼ cups blanched ground almonds

juice of 1 lemon

1 pinch of salt

½ teaspoon baking powder

Sift confectionary sugar with baking powder.

Add ground almonds.

Add juice of lemon.

Fold in stiffly beaten egg whites, gently.

Bake at 350 degrees for about 30 mins. or until toothpick comes out clean.

Spread bottom layer (night) with preserves, put on day layer, and frost entire torte with favorite icing.

JANE JENKINS

Jane and her husband, Jim Jenkins, are supporters of Aspen's arts groups and are always at the dances. Jane is also a poet and musician, giving musical programs at the Aspen Historical Society for children in the community.

ROMAN APPLE CAKE

1 cup sugar

1 cup brown sugar

1 cup butter

1 cup buttermilk

2 eggs well beaten

2½ cups cake flour

1 teaspoon baking soda

1 teaspoon baking powder

½ teaspoon salt

2 teaspoons cinnamon

2 cups apples

1 teaspoon vanilla

Cream shortening and add sugar. Add eggs. Alternate buttermilk and sifted flour and other dry ingredients which have been sifted together. Add apples.

Sprinkle with this topping mixture:

1 teaspoon cinnamon

½ cup sugar

½ cup nuts

Bake in greased 10x13 pan at 300 degrees for one hour.

MOLLY SWANTON AND CARLA PELTONEN

Molly and Carla write romance novels for Harlequin Books under the nom de plume of Lynn Erickson. They brainstorm the story-lines together and take turns writing the chapter. Some of their titles are **Sweet Nemesis**, **High County Pride**, **The Silver Kiss**.

KENTUCKY BUTTER CAKE

3 cups flour

¼ teaspoon soda

½ teaspoon baking powder

1 cup butter (or ½ margarine and ½ butter)

2 cups sugar

4 eggs

1 cup buttermilk

2 teaspoons vanilla

Butter Sauce:

1 cup sugar

¼ cup water

½ cup butter

1 teaspoon vanilla

Heat until melted.

Sift flour, salt, soda, and baking powder.

Cream butter, slowly add sugar, creaming well. Mix buttermilk and vanilla and eggs. Alternately add milk and flour mixture to creamed mixture, blending well after each addition.

Bake in 10" tube pan, greased on the bottom. Bake at 350 degrees for one hour or more until golden brown. Prick top with fork. Pour butter suace over cake. Cool. Remove pan and sprinkle with powdered sugar.

MARTIE STERLING

Martie is an author, humorist and travel photojournalist. She has monthly columns in **Ski Magazine** and **New Choices** magazine. She is very funny. She's also written a novel about Aspen entitled **Days of Stein and Roses.**

LEMON SOUFFLE

Martie says this is actually Pat Boyd's lemon souffle. She says Pat got it from a spy who came in from the cold. It's a dream dessert for all places and people. Martie says her dinner guests have eaten it 15 times...and asked for more.

1 tablespoon grated lemon rind

2/3 cup lemon juice (bottled is fine)

2 envelopes unflavored gelatin

½ cup water

6 eggs

1½ cups sugar

2 cups heavy cream

1. Grate lemon rind and have juice ready for step #5.

2. Sprinkle gelatin over water in small saucepan. Let stand 10 minutes until gelatin is softened. Place saucepan over very low heat until gelatin dissolves (mixture will be clear). Remove from heat and cool.

3. Combine eggs and sugar in large bowl of electric mixer. Beat mixture at high speed until very thick and light. (This will take 7-8 minutes.)

4. While eggs and sugar are beating, whip 1½ cups of cream in a small bowl until peaks form. Refrigerate.

5. Combine lemon rind and juice with cooled gelatin, pour into egg-sugar mixture. Continue beating until well blended.

6. Remove bowl from mixer. Chill about 5 minutes by placing bowl in large bowl partly filled with ice and water. Stir frequently just until mixture is thick enough to mound.

7. Fold in whipped cream. Pour into 2-quart dish... refrigerate at least 3 hours.

8. Beat remaining cream. Garnish souffle with cream and lemon wedges.

"The Aspen Eagle" by sculptor O. Louis Wille

MARGE HALLUM

Marge loves anything historical. She and her husband, Gus Hallum, live in the childhood Aspen home of Harold Ross, the founder and long-time editor of the **New Yorker Magazine**. Marge is also an authority on geneology and she is a volunteer with the Colorado Historical Society. She and Gus also own and operate the Deep Powder Ski Lodge. This is a luscious summer dessert.

WATERMELON FILLED WITH FRESH FRUIT

½ large watermelon

1 quart of strawberries

1 pint of raspberries

1 pint of blackberries

1 quart of orange or raspberry ice (optional. If not used, use more fruit.)

6 red plums

1 raw pineapple

several peaches

2 cups of sugar

1 cup of water

2 tablespoons Curacao

small bottle of chilled champagne

Cut two or three cupsful of watermelon balls with a large melon cutter and chill. With a large spoon remove the rest of the pulp from the melon, leaving a shell 1¼ inches thick.

Place shell in refrigerator.

Make syrup by boiling sugar and water for five minutes. Cool. When cold, pour a little on watermelon balls. Do the same with washed and stemmed fruit. Chill for several hours.

Sprinkle pineapple with powdered sugar.

Remove watermelon from refrigerator and put orange or raspberry ice in the center.

Mash the orange or raspberry ice over the bottom and sides of the watermelon shell. Arrange different prepared fruits in circles, alternating the light-colored with the dark-colored...reserve the center for the sliced peaches which must be sliced and sweetened at the last moment.

Sprinkle the edge of the watermelon shell generously with confectioner's sugar to give a frosted look. Sprinkle top with blanched almonds.

The well-chilled champagne with which the Caracao has been mixed may be poured on just before serving. This will serve 16.

310

A place to write your recipes

A place to write your recipes

A place to write your recipes

INDEX TO RECIPES

INDEX TO PEOPLE